Anna Wolfrom Dove

AND THE WIGWAM THE TEA ROOM

The Remarkable Single Woman Homesteader and the History of Her Legendary Tea Room in the Rocky Mountains

Nina Jones Kunze

D1518505

Anna Wolfrom Dove and The Wigwan Tea Room: The Remarkable Single Woman Homesteader and the History of Her Legendary Tea Room in the Rocky Mountains

Managing Editor and Alchemist: Robin Shukle
Design: Liz Mrofka, What If? Publishing
Cover Images: John Reichhardt private collection.
Printed by: CreateSpace

Nina Jones Kunze
Fort Collins, Colorado

ISBN-13: 9781070836454

Anna's Majestic cookstove, used for baking treats at the Wigwam. Sketch by Judy Meyers.

Table of Contents

THE WIGWAM AND ESTES CONE
WIND RIVER TRAIL — ESTES PARK, COLO.

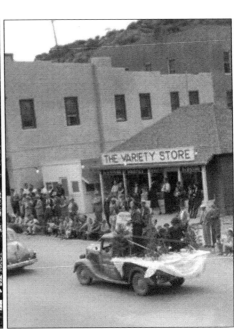

Author's Note

Anna Wolfrom is often referred to as the "First Single Woman Homesteader in the Estes Valley," having earned her Homestead Patent in 1914. While this isn't technically true because Ida McCreery was single when she earned her Homestead Patent for land on Devil's Gulch near Estes Park in 1899, the McCreery family had a lot of involvement in earning the patent, too. By the time Ida received title to the land, her family had been working the acreage and spending summers there for 23 years.

So, a more accurate title for Anna Wolfrom would be "The First Independent Woman Homesteader in the Estes Valley."

A few other brave single women followed Ida and Anna's lead in claiming land in the Estes Valley area. Historians presumed that Anna's success as the first independent woman homesteader inspired those who followed her to attempt the same success.

The single women who filed homestead claims in the Estes Valley area after Anna were Esther Burnell (who later married Enos Mills), Katherine Garetson, and Amanda Blocker Byrd. The reduction of the requirement to three years in 1909 made "proving up" on a homestead a little less challenging than the five years that had been required when Anna earned her claim. Despite that, the only single woman in the Estes Valley besides Anna Wolfrom and Ida McCreery who successfully gained her homestead patent was Katherine Garetson.

All of these women have fascinating stories, but Katherine was the only single woman homesteader in the area to write extensively about her experiences and challenges in earning her homestead patent. Her family members kept the manuscript she wrote, and the Allenspark Wind published her memoir *Homesteading Big Owl* in 1989, and an updated version in 2012. Katherine's account gives us an important reference about the hardships and joys of earning a homestead claim in a mountain environment, many of the same ones that Anna Wolfrom undoubtedly experienced.

The McCreery family in front of their homestead cabin, which they moved into in May of 1876. Note the sod roof. This cabin is still standing on McCreery land. **From left to right:** Bertha, Elbert, William H., Ida and Mabel McCreery.

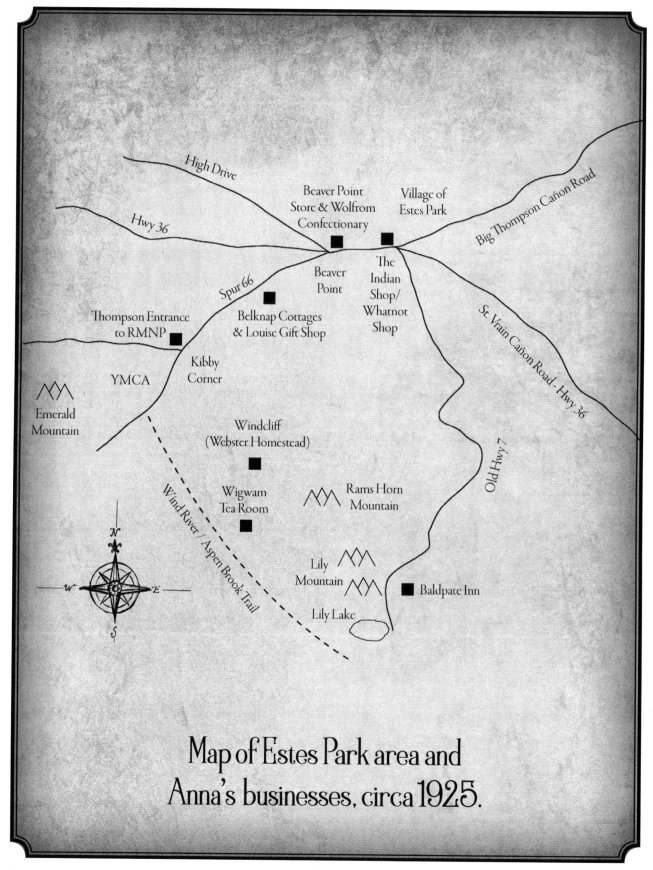

High Drive

Beaver Point
Store & Wolfrom
Confectionary

Village of
Estes Park

Big Thompson Cañon Road

Hwy 36

Beaver
Point

The
Indian
Shop/
Whatnot
Shop

Spur 66

Belknap Cottages
& Louise Gift Shop

St. Vrain Cañon Road - Hwy 36

Thompson Entrance
to RMNP

Kibby
Corner

YMCA

Emerald
Mountain

Windcliff
(Webster Homestead)

Old Hwy 7

Wind River / Aspen Brook Trail

Wigwam
Tea Room

Rams Horn
Mountain

Lily
Mountain

Baldpate Inn

Lily Lake

N
W E
S

Map of Estes Park area and
Anna's businesses, circa 1925.

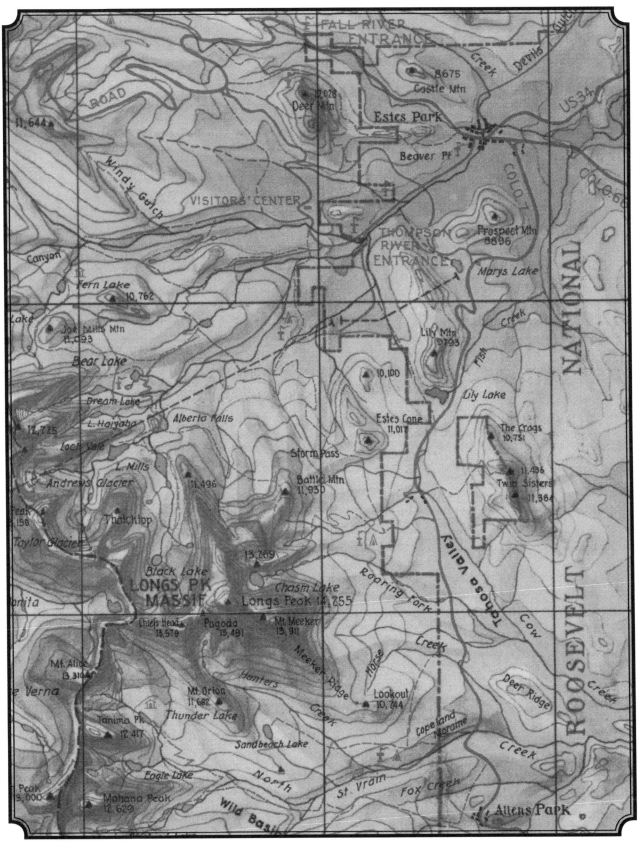

Colorado Centennial 1859-1959, relief map of Rocky Mountain National Park compiled, drawn and published by J.M. Sprecher, P.E., Cartographer 1959.

Foreword

Lily Mountain towers above the acreage Anna Wolfrom homesteaded, and is a favorite place of mine. The trailhead to the top is about ¼ mile north of Lily Lake on State Highway 7 near Estes Park, Colorado. It traverses the east side of Lily Mountain at a level grade for the first mile or so, offering sweeping views of the Estes Valley, the Cheley Camp area, and the Baldpate Inn, which sits on the shoulder of Twin Sisters Mountain. When you reach the north end of Lily Mountain, the trail takes a sharp left and begins to ascend more steeply, zig-zagging within a forest of lodgepole pine, until you reach the base of the boulders that define the top of the mountain. It takes some scrambling to get to the top, but within a few minutes you are able to take a seat on a flat rock with enough room for three or four clusters of hikers, and enjoy your lunch or snack with a dramatic view of Longs Peak, Estes Cone, the Continental Divide, and the Mummy Range.

And if you look straight down from the west side of this summit, you'll see a tiny green roof in the woods. That's the Wigwam Tea Room, built about 1910. It's Anna Wolfrom's first business, still standing on land that was purchased in 1989 for inclusion into Rocky Mountain National Park. There's no visible road leading to the cabin, which makes it seem an odd location. A curious person who's never heard of Anna would wonder what it's doing there, seemingly in the middle of nowhere.

On a recent day after I hiked to the top of Lily Mountain, I was leaning over the edge, taking photographs of the Wigwam, and a young mother with her two children, a boy and a girl of about 8 or 10, were admiring the views with her. I pointed to it and said, "See that green rooftop down there? That's the cabin of Anna Wolfrom Dove, the first single woman homesteader in the Estes Valley."

"Really?" the woman said.

The kids peered into the abyss and said, "Wow!"

Those visitors were one of a very few who ever come to the area and learn about Anna Wolfrom Dove and the Wigwam Tea Room.

I owned a home in Estes Park and was a part time resident for 20 years before I ever heard about Anna or the Wigwam. When I finally did, I was intrigued, fascinated to learn more, and mesmerized with what I found out.

Anna's life is a buried secret, an important one that needs to be unearthed. There's little detail about her life in the archives and books about the history of the Estes Valley. I hope that changes. People who visit Estes Park and fall in love with the place need to know about this plucky woman and what she achieved.

Anna was a remarkable and educated woman, who had a lifetime of unusual achievements, as a courageous and successful homesteader, a published author of some dozen books and plays, a savvy businesswoman with multiple businesses, an accomplished cook, real estate investor, art and Indian Artifact collector, devoted daughter, sister, and aunt, (and eventually, wife), philanthropist, mentor and friend to her many employees, customers, and neighbors. A single woman homesteader was an oddity, perhaps dismissed by most because of the unusual nature of her undertakings. Is that why nobody seemed to take note of her?

Researching and preserving the history of Anna Wolfrom Dove became a passion for me. Without recording her history, knowledge of her life slips away and she is forgotten. The little we know about her was preserved by the very thinnest thread of luck and chance. If I've learned one thing by writing this book, it's that important history can slip away far too easily.

Learning about Anna's life could be galvanizing for women and girls who might someday achieve things that take the kind of courage and wisdom that Anna displayed. Women today are still working toward being accepted in our culture as equals to men. Yet this adventurous woman struck out on her own over a century ago and made a life in the Colorado wilderness. I have learned a lot about bravery and fortitude from researching Anna's life, and I hope you will be as inspired by her as I am.

Current day view of the Wigwam as it looks from the top of Lily Mountain, with the Mummy Range in the background. The Windcliff development is on the right, and the YMCA of the Rockies is in the center.

Acknowledgements

Gathering the information for and writing the story of Anna Wolfrom Dove and the Wigwam Tea Room was only possible with the cooperation and support of many people.

First and foremost, without the trust and unwavering support from John and Ann Reichhardt, telling this story would never have been possible. John's initial research about Anna Wolfrom Dove in the 1980s and 90s was the foundation upon which this story was built. Karen Reichhardt was generous in sharing her memories of the Wigwam and helping me understand what a special place it is.

Adding to the story, Jak Wolfrom was helpful in providing photos and more detail about the Wolfrom family history. The staff at the Estes Park Museum, Derek Fortini and Jessica Michak, Carie Essig, curator of the Lula M. Dorsey Museum at the YMCA of the Rockies, Maggie Malone at the Panhandle Plains Museum in Canyon, Texas, and Kelly Cahill, Curator of the Rocky Mountain National Park Archive Collection, all provided material that contributed.

Many others helped by contributing their memories, their photos, their art or their knowledge:

Sarah Donohoe, Curt Buchholtz, Vaughn Baker, George Leonard, Melissa Strong, Vic Hoerner, Pamalah Tipps, Linda McCreery, Sue Lamb, Bobbie Heisterkamp, Keith Pritchard, Dennis Reinke, Sarah Sullivan, and Susan Skog.

My readers improved the book with their editing suggestions. Laura Pritchett, Jim Pickering, Marcia Meredith Hensley, and Cory LaBianca all had important contributions.

My publishers, Liz Mrofka and Robin Shukle of What If? Publishing gave me sound guidance and an excellent book design.

My Dad, William Jones, motivated me in the earliest stages to begin this project with his example and his encouragement.

And I'm so appreciative of Scott Kunze, my husband, who has solidly supported this project from the beginning. He continues to be an enthusiastic promoter of my book.

I'm grateful to all of you for the time you took to help me understand and piece together the story of Anna Wolfrom Dove. Thank you.

1
CHAPTER

An Unconventional Pioneer

Anna Wolfrom didn't know when she filed her homestead claim in the woods near Estes Park, Colorado, that the challenges of "proving up" would include mastering the use of a hammer, axe and shovel. The hardships of homesteading at an elevation of 8,250 feet included a short growing season, rocky infertile soil, and relentless, extreme winter winds and cold. Add to that the burden of never ending work and surely, there were times when it seemed impossible.

Anna came to Estes Park to homestead alone in the days before most women stepped out of the mold. She was not a meek, compliant woman; some

a modest filing fee and claim 160 acres if they improved the land and resided on it for seven months out of each year for five years. Improving the land generally required the building of a structure and making the land productive in some way, usually by cultivating. Allowing women to homestead had the caveat that she be the "Head of Household," so that if she were to marry, ownership would revert to her husband.[1]

In 1909, the Homestead Act was revised, and the residency requirement was decreased to three years, still permitting an absence of five months each year.[2]

Anna was a single schoolteacher from Kansas City, an unlikely candidate for successfully earning a homestead patent in the wild Rocky Mountains, as she was accustomed to a cultured and comfortable life.

would call her an eccentric spinster. But she was on a mission. In 1907, she moved to Colorado to homestead 160 acres of land, just weeks after graduating at age 35 from the University of Missouri with a degree in Liberal Arts. Graduating from college that late in life was also remarkable in that day and age, but Anna had her reasons.

According to the Homestead Act of 1862, any Head of Household (man or woman) could pay

Anna was a single schoolteacher from Kansas City, an unlikely candidate for successfully earning a homestead patent in the wild Rocky Mountains, as she was accustomed to a cultured and comfortable life. Anna's work had always been in the classroom or behind a desk as a student or a writer, instead of pushing a heavy wheelbarrow full of supplies or hauling water for dishes, laundry and bathing.

Aerial photo of what was known in Anna's day as the Wind River Valley, by Lew Dakan. Twin Sisters is the mountain at the top, with Lily Lake just below it. The winding roads on the bottom left are in Windcliff Estates, and Anna's homestead is just above the Windcliff Road that loops farthest to the right.

The Wind River Valley was a spectacular choice for Anna, and her 160 acre parcel sat just below Ram's Horn Mountain (then called Sheep Mountain) and Lily Mountain, about ¼ mile south of today's Windcliff Estates, near the end of Spur 66, about five miles south of Estes Park. It had a sweeping view of the Mummy Range to the north, and towering above to the east were the rugged rock outcroppings of Lily Mountain and Teddy's Teeth. A stream called Aspen Brook flowed through the property. The meadows of mountain grasses had a rich sprinkling of wildflowers including scarlet paintbrush, wild geraniums, yarrow, and aspen daisies. At the edge of the meadows and along the hillsides were ponderosa and lodgepole pine trees, aspen groves, and many rugged rock formations spotted with lichen in bright chartreuse, chestnut and copper.

Influenced by friends already living in the Estes Valley, a dream took hold in Anna's heart of escaping the drudgery of city life in exchange for life in a pine-scented forest, next to a melodious brook and craggy mountain peaks. Anna succeeded because she was resourceful, yes. But she also had a deep abiding love of the Estes Valley and of her little piece of that paradise.

Estes Park, at that time, was a dusty village with just a smattering of homes and businesses. Besides the post office, businesses included a drugstore, steam laundry, barbershop and a few hotels. The year Anna filed her claim, around 320 people received mail in Estes Park, which had an estimated population of about 500.[3]

In the beginning, Anna's task was to build a simple claim cabin, as required by the Homestead Act of 1862. She hired help from a neighbor, most likely Jimmy Fields, who lived just south of her, a little further up Aspen Brook. Jimmy lived in a shack at the edge of a meadow. He was a homesteader who was described as a miner and a trapper, a friendly sort who gave neighbor children rides on his burro, and who wintered at the Hupp Hotel in Estes Park Village.

Jimmy Fields, Anna's helper and closest neighbor, on his burro.

Anna and her neighbor hauled lumber, nails, and shingles in a wheelbarrow from where the road ended, about two miles from her cabin. Manual labor of this kind was new to Anna at first. She suffered from blisters on her hands, an aching back, and crushing fatigue. Undeterred, she eventually learned how to use the hammer and saw, and once Jimmy's help was finished, she put the shingles on the roof herself.[4]

Daytime dress for women in 1907 included an A-line dark skirt that fell just above the ankle, a white or light cotton high-necked blouse, and a corset underneath to accentuate the waist. After lunch on summer afternoons, proper ladies would wear pastel-colored dresses, usually with lace trim around the bodice, sleeves or skirt. Cotton stockings and boots with buttons were also part of the style.

Anna's backbreaking effort building her homestead cabin had to be hampered by the flowing fabric of her long skirt, and the stockings oppressive. Who knows, maybe she tossed aside convention and wore slacks when shoveling, hauling, and hammering. And surely during the days when she was gathering firewood, hauling water, or pulling weeds in her garden, the clothing she wore was more practical than a pastel cotton dress.

Whatever garments she wore, Anna washed them and any household linens in a large tub, rubbed by hand against a metal washboard. Wringing out each item by hand involved twisting and squeezing out the water, then shaking out remaining drops and pinning each one to a clothesline, taking care to bring them inside before the afternoon thunderstorms rolled in.

The claim cabin was tiny, just large enough for a small bed and table, providing shelter from summer thunderstorms and wind. Anna had a meager amount of money to improve the land, but this modest dwelling fulfilled the requirement.

———◆———

Probably out of necessity, Anna continued to teach for several years after filing her homestead claim. But she was ready for something new, and the entry in her diary on May 30, 1904 says:

"Leaving Kansas City on the rear end of the vestibule train, I saw for the first time in several months the green verdure of the spring that took my heart and mind out of the past months of imprisonment. In speaking of my teaching as imprisonment I do not want to say I despise it. Quite the contrary. Only the long months of the cold winter, the long struggle with the child mind to live and keep the beautiful world about them is laborous."

Filing a homestead claim in spectacular Estes Park in 1907 no doubt made her life as a school-teacher seem all the more tedious. Despite the monotony, Anna returned to Kansas City each fall to teach school and earn the money that was essential to support herself and her homestead.

It's unclear how Anna was able to successfully prove up her Colorado claim while continuing to teach in Kansas City, when an absence of only five months per year was allowed in order to gain the Homestead Patent. Perhaps those who investigated the validity of claims for the government land office were more lenient for those in such remote locations.

That left a few short summer months to make improvements to her claim cabin, and to build the larger cabin next to it that would eventually become the Wigwam Tea Room. Those first years were undoubtedly very busy and challenging.

COURTESY JOHN REICHHARDT.

Anna's claim cabin. This is the first structure Anna built in order to fulfill the requirements of making a homestead claim.

Anna's teaching career was long and varied, and she continued to instruct students in Kansas City until 1921. Anna taught at various schools in Kansas City, including Central High School, The Yeager School, and Northeast High School. She was trained to teach a variety of subjects, and various accounts tell of her teaching French, History, English, Drama, and Math.

Anna said in a newspaper interview that she asked for a leave of absence from teaching in 1912-13, but she went back to teaching the next year.[5]

Anna had an engaging personality, and her students were fond of her. She had a strong friendship with one student in particular, William Powell, who became a Hollywood legend in the 1930s. He was most famous for his starring role in "The Thin Man" in 1934, with Myrna Loy. The movie was nominated for four Academy Awards, and was so popular that five sequels followed in the 1930s and 1940s.[6] William and Anna exchanged Christmas cards and letters for years, and he visited her at her homestead.[7]

Her homestead, though, was far from secure. Leaving it behind for the long winter months left it vulnerable to human or animal intruders. Her cabin was now more substantial and worth protecting. From the beginning, Anna knew that she would need more room than the tiny claim cabin provided, and soon after it was completed, she built a larger cabin that could be inhabited year-round. By 1910, the new cabin was completed, with a fieldstone fireplace and chimney, and a covered porch.

Soon afterward, Anna began informally serving refreshments to summertime hikers and horseback riders traveling the Wind River Trail to or from Longs Peak or Lily Lake. Hikers were always hungry and thirsty.

When Anna learned her land was in danger of being taken over by claim jumpers, she took a break from her teaching job at Central High School and stayed on her homestead the winter of 1912-13.

Anna kept a diary from May 1904 to September of 1906 which has been preserved. She was between 32 and 34 years old then, and the diary covers just a sliver of time in a long and eventful life. If she recorded her experiences while she lived in Estes Park, they were lost. By all indications, most of the writing she did was on her fictional books and plays, rather than writing about her own life. How fascinating it would be if she'd kept a diary during her homesteading years! But undoubtedly she was so busy with endless tasks during those years, she didn't get much writing done.

The diary was from a different time in her life, when she traveled a lot. She enjoyed a close relationship with her brother Philip, and most of the emotional detail in her diary is about her grief over his illness and death. In it, she also gives brief details of her travels to Ireland, England, France, Norway, Sweden, Denmark, and Germany. Toward the end she describes returning to Missouri and enrolling at the University of Missouri, in her final year of college, just before she moved to Estes Park and filed her homestead claim. The diary is part of the collection of the Estes Park Museum today.

She lived alone in her remote cabin, with just the company of her cat, dog, horse and chickens, determined to protect what she had worked so hard for. She had also built a simple barn to give shelter to her horse and chickens.

Winter living on her homestead, alone with no electricity, running water, or central heat was full of challenges. Just feeding herself and staying warm took up most of the day. She may have switched to longer-lasting coal for her winter fuel in the Majestic Stove, her only source of heat besides the fireplace. She heated hot water for bathing in the sidearm of her Majestic.

But she relished the time alone, and she spent many hours reading and writing, undoubtedly sitting in the kitchen next to the stove, with a kerosene lantern burning for light. Winter winds can be relentless in the Estes Valley, and in Anna's day, I'm sure those winds whistled through the cracks between the logs of her cabin walls.

On December 1, 1912, a heavy storm hit that raged for five days and nights, burying the area with several feet of snow. Accounts vary as to whether it was five or seven feet deep. Either way, that sort of snow depth created immense hardship. It was four days before Anna could shovel her way as far as her barn to check on her animals.

For twelve long days, Anna was marooned in her cabin. Meanwhile, in the village of Estes Park, men began to organize a rescue mission, and formed small groups to check on residents in outlying areas. This party of Good Samaritans brought food and supplies to stranded folks, but when they reached Anna, they saw that she had provisioned herself well for such an event, and she was safe and well-fed amidst an astonishing amount of snow. According to Anna, "they found me snug and warm, for I had provided for emergencies like that. I had packed my Wigwam with fuel and food, and I was all right."[8]

When her rescuers came, she had to leave her horse and chickens behind, traveling to town on snowshoes. Her neighbor Jimmy Fields was probably

Anna's skis, which she hung on the side of the Wigwam after having to use them until May after the epic snowstorm of December 1912.

the trapper she mentioned as the one who fed her animals until a trail could be forged through the snowdrifts to get the animals to a nearby ranch. Anna was not able to return to her homestead until March because of deep snow. When she did return, she had to use skis until the end of May.[9] To commemorate the winter of such big snow, she hung the skis on the side of the Wigwam when summer finally came. The Estes Park Museum has that pair of skis in their collection today.

That epic storm caused extensive damage in Estes Park. At the YMCA, the dining hall roof collapsed under the heavy load, smashing dishes and glassware to bits. Travel throughout the Estes Valley and beyond ground to a halt and people were stranded for days, making food and consumables scarce.

Four days after the storm, several men headed toward Lyons with two wagons and several saddle horses to replenish supplies. The snow was still impossibly deep, so they had to ride the horses in circles in front of the wagons to forge a passable path. Eventually they met up with men who were digging their way toward Estes from Lyons.[10]

The United States of America,

To All To Whom These Presents Shall Come, Greeting:

a Certificate of the Register of the Land Office at Denver, Colorado

Denver 06719 } **Whereas,** has been deposited in the General Land Office

whereby it appears that, pursuant to the Act of Congress of May, 1862, "TO SECURE HOMESTEADS TO ACTUAL SETTLERS ON THE PUBLIC DOMAIN," and the Acts supplemental thereto, the claim of _Anna Wolfram_ has been established and duly consummated, in conformity to law, for the

west half of the southeast quarter of Section ten and the west half of the northeast quarter of Section fifteen in Township four north of Range seventy - three west of the Sixth Principal Meridian, Colorado, containing one hundred sixty acres.

according to the Official Plat of the Survey of the said Land, returned to the General Land Office by the Surveyor General:

NOW KNOW YE, That there is, therefore, granted by the **UNITED STATES** unto the said _claimant_ the tract of Land above described: TO HAVE AND TO HOLD the said tract of Land, with the appurtenances thereof, unto the said _claimant_ and to _the of the said claimant_ heirs and assigns forever; subject to any vested and accrued water rights for mining, agricultural, manufacturing or other purposes, and rights to ditches and reservoirs used in connection with such water rights, as may be recognized and acknowledged by the local customs, laws and decisions of Courts; and there is reserved from the Lands hereby granted a right of way thereon for ditches or canals constructed by the authority of the United States.

IN TESTIMONY WHEREOF, I, _Woodrow Wilson_ President of the United States of America, have caused these letters to be made patent, and the Seal of the General Land Office to be hereunto affixed.

GIVEN under my hand, at the City of Washington, the _eighteenth_ day of _April_ in the year of our Lord One Thousand _nine_ Hundred and _fourteen_ and of the Independence of the United States the One Hundred and _thirty - eighth._

BY THE PRESIDENT: _Woodrow Wilson_

By _M. P. LeRoy_ Secretary.

L. Q. C. Lamar Recorder of the General Land Office.

Recorded, _Patent Number 399005_

Filed for Record the _23_ day of _May_ A. D. 1914 at _8 30_ o'clock _A_ M.

A. P. Green Recorder

By _F. C. Alford_ Deputy

Anna's Homestead Patent, dated April 27, 1914, giving her title to 160 acres of land. Obtained from the Larimer County Courthouse.

Anna eventually spent many winters alone in her cabin. "I was never lonesome or afraid," she said. "These mountains have always been safe for any woman. The men who lived here then were few but they were princely in their behavior toward women. They went to great lengths to help when opportunities or necessity presented the chance. My long winters gave me the much coveted time to do some writing. I like to write books and plays, and I had plenty of time in which to indulge my fancy.

"During the winter, mountain sheep, coyotes, deer and other wild animals came around to my cabin door, but I was never afraid of them. I had my dog, cat and all my books to keep me company and they proved adequate."[11]

Anna grew used to staying through the winters alone on her homestead and did so for years. One fall, friends who were concerned for her safety implored Anna to move into town for the season. By then, Anna owned property in the village of Estes Park. So, she fixed herself a room with a bath in a building she owned in town. But, as she described it, "I would awaken at night with such a longing for this mountain home that I did not stay there for long."[12]

Anna's resourcefulness was likely the cause of her success, but she probably succeeded also because of her deep love of the Estes Valley and her little piece of that paradise. Anna was awarded her homestead patent on April 18, 1914.

Sketch of Anna's claim cabin by Judy Meyers.

1. Hensley, Marcia Meredith, *Staking Her Claim: Women Homesteading the West.* Glendo, WY: High Plains Press, 2008.

2. The National Archives, https://www.archives.gov/education/lessons/homestead-act

3. Pickering, James H., *This Blue Hollow: Estes Park, the Early Years, 1859-1915.* Niwot, CO: University Press of Colorado, 1999.

4. Marshall, Mrs. T.P. "Woman Runs Tea Shop on Side of A Mountain: City-Bred Girl Won by Rockies," *Dallas Morning News, Sunday, October 5, 1924.*

5. "Playright (sic) and Proprietress of Curio Shop is M.U. Graduate," *The Columbia Evening Missourian*, Columbia, MO, Dec. 20, 1921.

6. HollywoodsGoldenAge.com

7. Interview with Jak Wolfrom, May 31, 2017.

8. Marshall, Mrs. T.P. "Woman Runs Tea Shop on Side of A Mountain: City-Bred Girl Won by Rockies," *Dallas Morning News, Sunday,* October 5, 1924.

9. "Wilderness Home of a Kansas City School Teacher," *Kansas City Star*, June 14, 1924.

10. Jack and Lulabeth Melton, *YMCA of the Rockies: Reflections, Traditions and Vision*, Estes Park, CO: YMCA of the Rockies, 2006.

11. Marshall, Mrs. T.P. "Woman Runs Tea Shop on Side of A Mountain: City-Bred Girl Won by Rockies," *Dallas Morning News, Sunday,* October 5, 1924.

12. Ibid.

2
CHAPTER

Early Days Along Wind River

Anna Wolfrom was captivated by what she experienced when she first visited friends Frank and Cora Webster in Estes Park in 1905. Their homestead in what is now Windcliff Estates was less than a mile from what would eventually become Anna's homestead and the Wigwam Tea Room.

The corridor one traveled to reach the Webster's homestead (and later, Anna's) might seem like an afterthought compared to today's bustling downtown Estes Park and surrounds, but the Wind River area attracted some of the earliest residents and businesses, and soon became a popular place where many families built summer cottages.

Frank and Cora Webster on the front porch of their homestead cabin, which they named "Windcliff." Note the live evergreen branches on the front porch posts, showing how newly built the cabin was.

COURTESY WINDCLIFF.

Big Thompson Canõn* Road with stagecoach. Photo by Clatworthy.

Both Frank Lundy Webster and his wife Cora, and Guy LaCoste, another Estes Valley homesteader, were influential in Anna's decision to choose the Wind River Valley for her own homesteading adventure. Both Webster's and LaCoste's stories are part of the fabric of this area.

Webster, a newspaperman from Denver, first visited the Estes Park area in 1896. Despite his responsibilities as a journalist, he decided he must have a piece of this paradise. He learned that land was available to homestead on Sheep Mountain, above Highway 66. This was about five miles from the tiny village of Estes Park.

In 1897, Frank filed his homestead claim for 160 acres of land on the side of Sheep Mountain (now called Ram's Horn) which had magnificent views of the Continental Divide. Frank and his bride Cora built a homestead cabin, harvesting logs from the land, which was no easy feat on the steep terrain that was sparsely wooded. They named their cabin "Windcliff." The upscale development that's there today still bears that name, and the Webster's original homestead cabin still stands.

Frank dreamed of residing on the land full time and eventually operating a cattle ranch, a dream he never realized. His duties as editor of the Sunday *Denver Times* kept him in the city, and he was only able to live on his homestead occasionally. Soon after filing his claim, he married Cora King, who was also enthusiastic about the beautiful mountain setting, and she joined him in the effort to prove up his claim. Frank's reporting work required him to be in Denver or traveling the West much of the time.

The Estes Park Transportation Company, owned by F.O. Stanley, in downtown Estes Park.

Big Thompson Canõn* Road with Stanley Steamer. Photo by C.L. McClure.

So, during the years when residency was required to acquire the land, Cora stayed on the property.[13]

Imagine the difficulty in those years of commuting regularly from Denver by train to Lyons, and then by horse-drawn buggy to the homestead. The trip on the stagecoach from Lyons to Estes Park was six-and-a-half hours on a dusty, bumpy one-lane narrow road that was just a few feet from the river and not much higher, making the commute a very long day. Today's highway engineers would cringe at the old road's proximity to the river.

A few years later in 1907, The Loveland-Estes Park Automobile Company owned by David Osborn and his sons was the first to begin bringing travelers by automobile to Estes Park (then referred to as "The Park") and Rocky Mountain National Park. They owned three five-passenger touring Stanley Steamers.

Freeland O. and his twin brother Francis E. Stanley built their first Stanley Steamer in 1896, and by 1901 they had redesigned the automobile and began to produce larger quantities for commercial sale. Shortly thereafter, realizing how difficult the travel up the steep canyon roads was for the typical "horseless carriage" to navigate, they invented the Mountain Wagon, with more horsepower in its powerful steam engine that was replenished on the way to Estes Park by water from the nearby St. Vrain or Big Thompson River. The largest of the Mountain Wagons could transport as many as eleven people.[14]

Transportation by automobile took far less time than by horse-drawn carriage; in the steamers the trip up the canyon took three hours or less.[15] This new mode of transportation was wildly popular, and by 1908, F.O. Stanley had established the Estes Park Transportation Company, with service between Longmont and Estes Park through Lyons.[16]

⟹◆⟸

In 1901, *The Denver Times* merged with the *Rocky Mountain News,* and the reorganization cost Frank his job, despite his having performed very capably. But he was unemployed for only a day, because *The Denver Post* hired him immediately to write feature articles for their Sunday edition. Frank's articles were noteworthy because he didn't write local stories. He traveled extensively on horseback seeking stories, and his articles were always accompanied by photographs that Frank took himself.

A Lawrence, Kansas newspaper described the remote areas Frank traveled to for his stories. Sometimes he slept on the ground "in some prospector's tent, eating coarse grub in a railroad camp, following the surveyors on a great irrigation project, spending days in an Indian camp in New Mexico or climbing the mountain side to timberline to some new mine . . . his energy is boundless, and seems absolutely without limitations. His writings are marked with a grace and polish which have always been characteristic of the man, and in addition they have acquired a strength, virility and power that partakes of the ruggedness of the mountain and broad freedom of the open plains."[17]

Frank's work often took him far away from Estes Park. In 1903, he traveled to New Mexico as a representative of *The Denver Post,* to research residents' opinions on whether they preferred statehood singly or jointly with Arizona.[18] In 1907, he and his colleague Alfred Patek traveled to Panama to study the Panama Canal and take a series of photographs. They later used the photographs for lectures on a tour of the US about the progress of the Panama Canal. Both Webster and Patek were noted and respected for their skill as speakers on the lecture circuit.[19] Frank earned the title during those years of the "Best Newspaperman in the West."

Despite his demanding job requirements, Frank worked hard when he could to make improvements on his claim. He and Cora found it challenging to meet the necessary requirements to be awarded their homestead patent. Usually cultivation of the land is part of the requirement, and they were excused from this by providing sworn testimony that the land was not suitable for growing anything. Written affidavits by Frank and some of his neighbors helped document the fact that he had fulfilled the requirements, and he and Cora were awarded the Homestead Patent on November 5, 1904.

A few years later, the Schobinger family from Chicago discovered the area and were enamored because it reminded them of their homeland of

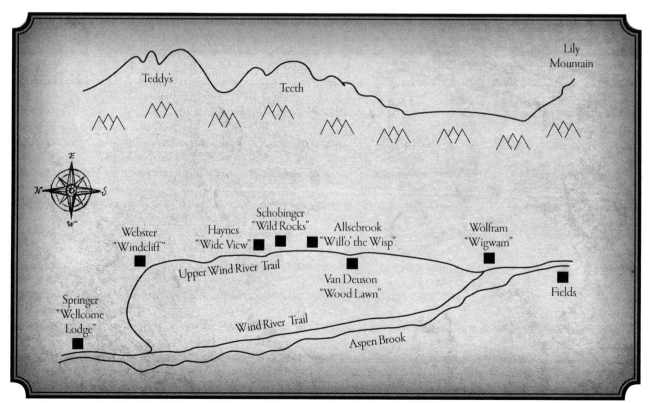

Map of the homes along Wind River Trail, circa 1922. Adapted from a map drawn by Elaine Hostmark Allsebrook.

Businesses at the Crossroads, also known as Kibby Corner, next to the Thompson Entrance to Rocky Mountain National Park.

The Holland Inn on the left (now the Dunraven Inn), along with other businesses at the Crossroads/Kibby Corner. This was next to the Thompson River Entrance to Rocky Mountain National Park, the main entrance to the national park until 1960 when the Fall River Entrance was opened.

Switzerland. The Schobingers convinced the Websters to sell them a one acre lot. They built a cabin and named it "Wild Rocks." That was the beginning of the Webster's Big Horn Park subdivision. The Websters subdivided and eventually created several other lots that they sold to other families, some of whom still have homes there: the Van Deusen's cabin was called "WoodLawn," the Haynes' named theirs "WideView," and the Allsebrook family decided upon "Will o' the Wisp" for theirs.[20]

Elaine Allsebrook Hostmark describes her family's purchase of an acre lot in 1919 for their cabin from Frank and Cora Webster as "pine forest and a scattering of aspen on the uphill (east) side and low sage and grass on the downhill (west) side, permitting the fantastic view of the Front and Mummy Ranges."

The families who settled in Webster's Big Horn Park had mail delivered to what Elaine called the "Crossroads," an intersection on Highway 66 where there was also a grocery store, gas pump, and a restaurant called the Holland Inn, now the Dunraven. At that time, an intersecting road led west and was the primary entrance into Rocky Mountain National Park. Elaine remembers walking to the "Crossroads" to retrieve their mail, which was carried in khaki drawstring bags, labeled "Allsebrook" in large letters drawn with a laundry pen that they had provided to the post office. Outgoing and incoming mail was carried in these bags, and one was traded for the other at the Crossroads, which later was commonly referred to as "Kibby Corner."[21]

⚬⟐⟐⟐⚬

Around the time that the Websters homesteaded Windcliff, Guy LaCoste, also a journalist, had filed a claim to Homestead 360 acres just two miles west, on what is now the YMCA of the Rockies property. Starting with a small dugout cabin, LaCoste soon completed a building he called the "Wind River Lodge" in 1902 on the slopes of what is now called Emerald Mountain, opening that same year for lodging to tourists. The lodge was stick built, with rustic pine siding, and the railings of the sweeping covered porches were made with whole trees. LaCoste also built a larger cabin next to the dugout, constructed from full logs. He used rough timber for siding on the gables. LaCoste's homestead had a stunning rugged mountain backdrop. The continental divide hugged the valley beyond the homestead, a semicircle of spectacular wilderness.

The old LaCoste homestead cabin is still standing amidst YMCA property, within a private inholding. The Wind River Lodge as it stood was demolished in 1977. However, an addition to the original building was preserved and is now the Lula Dorsey Museum at the YMCA.

LaCoste was a colleague of Webster's who was also employed at the *Denver Post*, and he was acquainted with Anna Wolfrom likely through her friendship with Frank Webster. But LaCoste had bigger ambitions than being an editor, and was willing to bend the rules and take big risks to attain his

Guy LaCoste, who homesteaded land on Wind River that is now part of the YMCA of the Rockies property.

Wind River Lodge, built by Guy LaCoste on what is now YMCA of the Rockies property.

goals. LaCoste circumvented the residency require-ments for homesteading by placing his parents on the Wind River land while he continued to work in Denver at the Post.[22]

LaCoste eventually gained title to almost 1,000 acres, and before the age of 30, he had made significant progress toward becoming one of the dominant landowners in the Estes Valley. Before constructing the Wind River Lodge, he had formed a partnership with two other Denverites and orga-nized the Estes Park Land and Investment Company,

with the goal of acquiring the Earl of Dunraven's substantial land holdings in the Estes Valley.

Dunraven had either lost interest or become too busy to pay any attention to his property in Estes Park. Encouraged by this, LaCoste and his partners attempted to negotiate with Dunraven's Denver lawyer without success. So, LaCoste decided that a trip abroad was necessary to present an offer directly to the Earl in England. He spent several weeks attempting to arrange a meeting with Dunraven. While in England, he contacted Anna Wolfrom,

Anna Wolfrom learned about Estes Park from LaCoste during that Christmas visit. Anna credited LaCoste with getting many others interested in filing homestead claims in the Estes Park area. No doubt during that visit in 1904, he filled Anna's head with images of the pristine mountain vistas, crystal clear streams and pine forests, and the future of Estes Park as a premiere tourist destination.

whom he had met previously, just before Christmas of 1904 and invited Anna to Christmas dinner. Instead, Anna invited La Coste to join her and a few fellow students for a home cooked holiday meal.

LaCoste was unusually bold and ambitious for a young man his age, as he had worked for his father in Denver during the 1890s at the Hampton-LaCoste Investment Company, where he became comfortable with risk taking and learned about leveraging money.[23] He told Anna he had come to Europe to "buy Estes Park."

Anna Wolfrom learned about Estes Park from LaCoste during that Christmas visit. Anna credited LaCoste with getting many others interested in filing homestead claims in the Estes Park area. No doubt during that visit in 1904, he filled Anna's

head with images of the pristine mountain vistas, crystal clear streams and pine forests, and the future of Estes Park as a premiere tourist destination. [24]

Anna had become intrigued with the Rocky Mountains before LaCoste's visit by hearing Dr. Isidor Loeb, who later became President of the University of Missouri, speak while she was a student there.[25] But undoubtedly her 1905 visit to the Webster Homestead, and the visit Guy LaCoste paid her while she was in England in 1904 contributed to her interest in the Estes Park area, and the idea of staking her own claim in the Colorado wilderness.

LaCoste worked diligently to negotiate with Dunraven for several years, eventually obtaining a lease with the option to purchase his land and hotel

The Windcliff Homestead cabin, as it looks today. This cabin was originally built by Frank Lundy Webster.

in early 1905. But he was unable to obtain the financing needed, and in the fall of that same year, he and his partners signed a quitclaim deed and relinquished their lease with option to buy to an Investment Company from Denver. By 1907 LaCoste had sold his shares of the Estes Park Land and Investment Company, and was rarely seen in Estes Park after that. LaCoste and his land grabbing schemes were history by the time Anna Wolfrom filed her Homestead Claim. Two years later LaCoste left the newspaper business and became a private secretary to Senator Charles J. Hughes, Jr.[26]

In 1909, the YMCA purchased the Wind River Lodge complex from the Estes Park Land and Investment Company for $8,500. The purchase included six buildings, including a seven room cot-

tage, a three room cottage, a tent cabin, 334 acres, and eleven head of horses. That year, the YMCA hosted their first conference, with most attendees staying in the Wind River Lodge. They pitched a large tent near the lodge and made it into a dining and meeting hall. The following year, the Wind River Lodge and its surrounding buildings were moved to the central YMCA campus, and plans proceeded to install a water and sewer system, build a dining hall and tent cottages. Once constructed, the dining hall was lit with brass kerosene lamps on the tables and hung from the ceiling.[27]

The view from the Windcliff Homestead, as it looks today. It's easy to see why Frank Webster chose this location.

It's unclear how they met, but Frank Webster and Anna Wolfrom had two things in common: a love of language, and a love of nature. The Websters had close friendships with many others who enjoyed writing and literature, and Frank exchanged letters with some friends that included critiques of one another's writing. Such friends included Enos Mills, Abner Sprague, and William Allen White.

Cora Webster was determined to live a refined life, despite the rugged and remote location of Windcliff. The Websters' home had china, fine linens, a Birdseye maple chest and dressing table, and even a piano. The Windcliff homestead had a barn to house horses and a buggy, and Cora rode sidesaddle in her long skirts when she explored the nearby forests and meadows, and used the horse-drawn buggy when she went to town for supplies. Anna had a close friendship with the Websters, who remained among her dearest friends until their deaths just weeks apart in late 1932.

The cabin Frank Webster built is still part of Windcliff Estates. It has been added onto but the old chimney from the original cabin is still visible. Visiting the location, you can easily get an idea of why the site appealed to Frank Webster. It has amazing, unobstructed views of the Continental Divide, now enjoyed by many who visit and live in Windcliff Estates, eventually developed by Don and Wylene Buser in the 1970s and 80s.

13. Buser, Wylene, *The Windcliff Story*, Estes Park, CO, self-published: undated.

14. Dunning, Harold Marion, *Over Hill and Vale, Volume III, History of Northern Colorado, Boulder, Colorado*, Johnson Publishing, 1971.

15. Jessen, Kenneth, *Estes Park Beginnings*, Loveland, CO, J.V. Publications, 2011.

16. Pickering, James H., *America's Switzerland: Estes Park and Rocky Mountain National Park, the Growth Years*, Boulder, CO, University Press of Colorado, 2005.

17. "Frank Webster is Making a Great Success in Colorado," *The Jeffersonian Gazette*, Lawrence, Kansas, April 30, 1903.

18. *The Santa Fe New Mexican*, January 8, 1903.

19. "Newspapermen to Go To Panama," *Oakland Tribune*, Oakland, California, March 11, 1907.

20. Hostmark, Elaine Allsebrook, *Allsebrooks in Estes Park*, Estes Park, CO, Unpublished, 1994.

21. Ibid.

22. Melton, Lulabeth & Jack, *YMCA of the Rockies: Seventy-Five Years of History 1907-1982*, Estes Park, CO, YMCA of the Rockies, 1982.

23. "Account of the Purchase of Estes Park," *Estes Park Trail*, April 24, 1941.

24. Ibid.

25. "Playright (sic) and Proprietress of Curio Shop is M.U. Graduate," *The Columbia Evening Missourian*, Columbia, MO, Dec. 20, 1921.

26. Pickering, James H., *This Blue Hollow: Estes Park, the Early Years, 1859-1915*, Niwot, CO: University Press of Colorado, 1999.

27. Jack and Lulabeth Melton, *YMCA of the Rockies: Reflections, Traditions and Vision*, Estes Park, CO: YMCA of the Rockies, 2006.

3
CHAPTER

A Tea Room in the Wilderness

A layer of dust coated Anna's long skirt and boots as she raised a pickaxe and with all her strength, brought it down on the remains of a tree stump. Jimmy Fields worked nearby, having tossed his leather vest aside and rolled up his sleeves. He paused and wiped his brow with his forearm. Then he stepped toward his burro and pulled at the lead, nudging the animal to strain further against a rope tied around a boulder, pulling it from the earth. Anna, having loosened the tree stump, began picking up melon-sized rocks and casting them to the side.

It was 1914, and they were clearing the way for the road to the Wigwam. It hadn't taken long for Anna to realize that a road was essential to her success. She had opened a tea room earlier that year.

By now, Anna was used to manual labor. When she was finished for the day, she would have to haul water from the stream up to her cabin and heat it in the sidearm of her stove before she could sink into a soothing warm bath.

We know for sure that Jimmy Fields was the laborer she hired to complete the road to the Wigwam, as it was mentioned in the *Estes Park Trail* in September 1914 that Anna had hired Jimmy and was completing the road at her own expense.

Hauling all of the supplies by wagon, wheelbarrow, horse or burro from where the road ended, up the path to the Wigwam was a burden. Everything had to be transported those last two miles: Flour, sugar, coffee, tea, and lard, as well as chocolate, nuts,

Anna Wolfrom on the porch of the Wigwam Tea Room

raisins and figs for candies and breads, along with essentials such as kerosene, ice, and milk. These supplies were needed to feed the steady stream of customers Anna was now serving at the Wigwam.

Anna's tea room became a success very quickly. Visitors were usually hot, ravenous and thirsty from hours on the trail, whether they were hiking or horseback riding. Anna was a big part of the attraction of the tea room. People started to spread the word, and her reputation and business grew.

She displayed a competent, yet friendly and welcoming style, with a contagious enthusiasm about her slice of paradise along Aspen Brook.

Anna's homestead had the advantage of being directly on the popular route traveled by hikers and horseback riders who were traveling between the YMCA Camp and Longs Peak or nearby destinations. In fact, Anna's Wigwam Tea Room was eventually part of the reason for the popularity of the trail along Aspen Brook.[28] The route's notoriety helped the Wigwam's business, but Anna had observed the growing prominence of the automobile and the trend toward outings with groups of people in passenger cars, often to roadside tea rooms. She knew that if a road led directly to her tea room, she would have even greater success.

As Anna had predicted, once she completed the road, more and more visitors came. Driving to a place like the Wigwam for an afternoon treat was a fashionable way to spend time.

During the first few summers before she earned her Homestead patent, hikers frequently stopped by Anna's cabin to rest, and she would always invite them in. A woman from Boston who, like many others, had stopped at Anna's property one summer afternoon, suggested that Anna begin serving tea. And so, in 1914, the year Anna received her patent, she officially opened her tea room, naming it the Wigwam.

According to Anna, "They used to come in and rest anyhow . . . the idea didn't seem so incongruous as it sounds at first. A tea room in the wilderness, on a trail that can only be traveled on foot or on horseback! It doesn't sound very practicable. But it is thoroughly so. There were days last summer which I served more than 200 people . . . there will be times when people in the big hotels down below find they can break their journey up the trail with tea and talk, they are not afraid to undertake it."[29]

The Wigwam had an inviting atmosphere, with Hopi, Zuni, or Navajo blankets on the walls, and Anna's collections from abroad adding warmth throughout the space. The fireplace was usually blazing except on the hottest summer days. Tables had centerpieces of wildflower bouquets, Wedgewood china, and unique glassware. Anna's kitchen windows had handmade ruffled curtains, and her floor had colorful rag rugs.

Anna's brother Philip had been an accomplished artist. After his death in 1904, Anna inherited a large collection of his animal sketches, many of which he drew during the years they both were students in Paris in the Latin Quarter. A gallery wall of Philip's animal art included a lion, tiger, zebra, donkey and buffalo, adding to the unique appeal of the Wigwam's interior. Anna eventually donated these prints to the Brooklyn Museum, and they are available there today for viewing online.

Early photo of Wigwam Tea Room visitors.

Sketch of Anna's stove in the Wigwam kitchen by Judy Meyers.

Zebra sketch by Philip Wolfrom that once hung in the Wigwam Tea Room.

Enamored by the beauty of the location, guests were so intrigued that they wanted to purchase Anna's wall decorations and the souvenirs and trinkets she had purchased during her time abroad in England, France and South America. With an enterprising spirit, Anna hatched the idea of a gift and curio shop to go along with the tea room, and she put her astute business head toward stocking items that would appeal to her tea room customers. As time went on, she began to specialize in Native American items, which were very popular in the Estes Park area. One of the methods she used to increase sales was to have a Native American present to demonstrate basket weaving when tourists stopped by to peruse her curio shop.

Anna likely served items such as Molasses Taffy, Brown Sugar Candy, Gingerbread, Sponge Cake, or French Biscuits. These items were all prepared on Anna's Majestic stove. Anna's fuel was wood in

Lion sketch by Philip Wolfrom that once hung in the Wigwam Tea Room.

COURTESY ESTES PARK MUSEUM.

Anna's Majestic stove, which she used to prepare treats for tea room guests, now in storage at the Estes Park Museum.

Soft Ginger Bread

1 cup sugar

1 cup butter or lard

1 cup molasses

4 cups flour

1 teaspoonful soda

1 teaspoonful each, ginger, cinnamon and cloves

3 eggs

Mix all the ingredients together and add 1 cup of boiling water.

—*M. Alberta Sprague*

COURTESY OF THE ESTES PARK MUSEUM.

From the "Tried & True Recipe Book," by the Estes Park PEO, Circa 1920.

THE WIGWAM AND ESTES CONE
WIND RIVER TRAIL — ESTES PARK, COLO.

COURTESY BOBBIE HEISTERKAMP.

The Wigwam with the new porch addition, from the Bobbie Heisterkamp postcard collection. The caption incorrectly states that the Estes Cone is behind the Wigwam. The Estes Cone is in fact further south, and not visible from the Wigwam.

summer months, and coal in winter when extra warmth was needed. An ongoing chore for Anna and her staff was gathering firewood, and each day before starting up the stove, they cleaned out and disposed of the previous day's ashes.[30]

Anna's stove was kept at the Notchtop Restaurant in Estes Park for years, long after the Wigwam's closure. When the Notchtop owners remodeled and needed to make room for more customers, they donated the stove to the Estes Park Museum.

Running the Wigwam boiled down to a lot of hard work. Anna likely rose each day before dawn to dress, then start a fire on the stove for breakfast, sweep the floors, make the bed, then feed the chickens, horse, cat and dog, and then begin to bake for that day's visitors to the tea room. In between guests, the afternoon might include weeding, ironing, washing dishes, dusting, mending, and mopping.

High altitude baking posed a unique challenge for a tea room owner. I've learned myself from living in Estes Park that baking cakes and breads is particularly tricky at an altitude of 8,000 feet. The altitude at the Wigwam is approximately 8,250 feet, but Anna managed to overcome any baking challenges, turning out excellent baked goods from her wood-fired Majestic.

In 1920, the local PEO Sisterhood chapter (Philanthropic Educational Organization) published a cookbook called the *Tried and True Recipe Book*, but by then Anna had been operating the Wigwam for years. Probably one of the tasks Anna took on after filing her homestead claim and before opening the tea room was the collecting, testing, modifying, and perfecting of recipes for high altitude. As anyone with baking experience knows, it is much more exacting than other types of cooking, and high altitude baking requires trial and error to avoid cakes with mushy centers and overdone edges. It's likely too that Anna traded baking secrets and recipes with the local members of the Estes Park Woman's Club, where she was a longtime member.

The Wigwam's success was of course a result of Anna's ingenuity, but it also had partly to do with the growing popularity of tea rooms, and partly to do with its unlikely yet handy location. People were surprised to come upon a tea room and curio shop after a hike through miles of forest.

A quaint cabin with such delightful refreshments in a spectacular setting aroused the enthusiasm of many a visitor. Guests were so charmed by the setting that they often wandered around the grounds after having refreshments, taking in the scenery or soaking their hot and dusty feet in Aspen Brook. Anna had created a business where visitors experienced the essence of a rustic mountain retreat along with refreshments as exquisite as you'd find in the finest city setting.

A Native American giving a basket weaving demonstration in front of the Wigwam.

44

28. Lynch, Henry. "Story of Miss Anna Wolfrom, Who Served 'Better' Teas and Cakes," *The Gentlewoman* circa 1923-24.

29. "A Woman's Tea House in the Wilderness," *Kansas City Star,* June, 1916.

30. "Cooking the Majestic Way," Smithsonian Libraries Blog, November 17, 2014, https://blog.library.si.edu

4
CHAPTER

The Tea Room Craze

At the turn of the 20th century, it was considered improper for a woman to dine out in an eating establishment unescorted by a man. But by the time Anna started her business in 1914, women in America had begun to demand change. At that point, just a few states had given women the right to vote (Wyoming in 1869, Colorado in 1893, Utah in 1895, and Idaho in 1896)[31]. The 19th Amendment to the U.S. Constitution would not be passed until 1920, giving women Universal Suffrage, but despite that, women were asserting their independence and influence. That growing very trendy and sought after. The new business model satisfied both women entrepreneurs who were longing for more creative expression and freedom, and women customers who were looking for a menu more to their liking. Instead of hearty meals featuring meat and potatoes catering to men with big appetites, tea room menus featured dainty sandwiches, wafers, salads and cakes. Tea rooms had become a stylish place for ladies to be. The popularity of tea rooms began to build in the early 1900s, and reached its peak in the 1920s. Opening the Wigwam in 1914, Anna's timing was spot on.[32]

Tea rooms had become a stylish place for ladies to be. The popularity of tea rooms begin to build in the early 1900s, and reached its peak in the 1920s. Opening the Wigwam in 1914, Anna's timing was spot on.

---

movement was one of a number of forces that had come together in the early 1900s, making tea rooms a popular, acceptable, and even desirable place for women to gather.

Not only did women flock to tea rooms, many dreamed of opening a tea room of her own, when in the not too distant past, it was frowned upon for a woman to run an eating establishment. Across the country, tea rooms with women proprietors were popping up everywhere, and they quickly became

Tea room décor was an important factor in business success. Atmosphere was what set tea rooms apart from other eateries with plain white walls and bright lighting. Tea rooms were always decorated as an expression of the owners' taste. The most successful ones had unusual décor, perhaps a bright orange wall with a lime green ceiling, and instead of heavy drapes, handmade calico curtains and rag rugs. Most skipped the formality of tablecloths and opted for the informality of placemats with paper napkins or even a bare table. This fit well in the Rocky Mountains, and the décor in Anna's and other mountain tea rooms leaned toward rustic, using elements from nature as a central theme.

Unique was the name of the game, as people were tired of the same old plain restaurants. The Wigwam was about as unusual a setting as you could find. I imagine Anna's décor at the Wigwam being eclectic. Articles about Anna and the Wigwam from Midwestern newspapers in the early 1900s described the Indian rugs and the zoo animal sketches by her brother Philip that gave character to the tea room. The time she spent in France and England likely influenced her taste, and any proper tea room in the early 1900s would have some frills, too. Anna had a Wedgewood China collection that lent a refined charm to the tea room.

Anna's tables surely had a sugar bowl filled with cut sugar or rock crystals and a pitcher of cream. On hot summer afternoons, iced tea was much more in demand than hot beverages, and without a freezer that conveniently made ice cubes in the right size, Anna and her staff would have had to break up a large block of ice with an ice pick. Anna likely bought ice blocks from the YMCA, which employees there cut to sell from a place on Wind River upstream from Dorsey Lake, on the Y grounds. [33]

The closest store to the Wigwam was the "Crossroads," then a bustling outpost of Estes, where today's Dunraven Inn and Swiftcurrent Lodge stand. There, residents picked up mail, groceries and gas. What we call "snail mail" today was the lifeline for many back then, including Anna, who surely looked forward to letters from her family. Anna and her staff probably made regular trips to the Crossroads, also called Kibby Corner, for milk and other items to stock the tea room.

During cool weather, Anna's staff served tea in a delicate china cup and saucer with a tea caddy, a teaspoon and a tea ball, or a china teapot. An alcohol lamp kept water boiling, and would be at a side table where trays of delectable sandwiches, cakes, biscuits, and candies were displayed. Coffee, either

A vintage tea room table.

hot or iced, was just as in demand as tea, and punch was also a popular option.

Balancing that, Anna's rustic dining furniture had probably been made from local trees with either wooden or bamboo seats, such as you see in historic photos of early Estes Park dining rooms. Native American items such as blankets, baskets, and woven trivets were increasingly an important part of the Wigwam décor as the curio shop flourished and the popularity of these items rose throughout the West.

Karen Reichhardt, whose family owned the Wigwam for many years after Anna's day, remembers

The Fall River Lodge dining room, decorated much like the Wigwam would have been.

48

The trail Anna's customers traveled to reach the Wigwam.

Punch - Six Quarts
Juice of 5 lemons
1 can of pineapple
Juice of 5 oranges
4 cups of sugar
1 pint of grape juice
6 quarts of water
Boil twenty minutes.
If in season, sliced cucumber, left in awhile to season it.
—*Alma Bond*

From the "Tried & True Recipe Book," by the Estes Park PEO, Circa 1920.

finding a postcard in Estes Park many years ago of the Wigwam tea room interior, showing an open, sunny room with large round tables that each featured a bouquet of sunflowers. But unfortunately, that postcard, or any other photo of the Wigwam interior from Anna's day, was never preserved.

Despite being called tea rooms, these American establishments didn't necessarily revolve around the serving of tea, the beverage, or tea as a meal. Lunchtime was the busiest, and most lucrative time to attract customers, and the Wigwam hosted many customers who had started their mountain outings early in the morning and by midday were ready for a feast.

Undoubtedly during her time in England, Anna witnessed the custom of adding flowers to butter in a jar screwed on tightly, which gave the butter a hint of floral taste and scent. Wildflowers were easily gathered in the meadows around the Wigwam, so this technique may have been used frequently to accent the treats at the Wigwam. Other unusual flavorings that were popular at the time were accompaniments such as a teaspoon of orange marmalade stirred into a piping hot cup of tea, or even a slice of pineapple with a wedge of lemon, stirred well.

In 1908 the mesh teabag had just been introduced. It didn't catch on right away, so Anna probably postponed adopting its use, opting instead for a metal ball as a tea infuser. By the late 1920s Anna likely served tea at the Wigwam using cloth tea bags when their popularity surged. Paper tea bags didn't come into common use until the 1950s.[34]

Prohibition became another force which helped fuel the tea room craze. Beginning in 1920, it changed the dynamic of the restaurant business. With alcohol outlawed, women found it easier to start a business without a large budget which would have been required to stock an extensive wine cellar and bar. Starting a tea room on a shoestring budget was possible, and many did so.

Tea rooms were a cultural phenomenon. Their popularity proved to the world that women were a class of customer with their own preferences, and that they had spending power. The tea rooms of the 1920s were much different in style and in menu offerings from the typical restaurant which had previously catered to men. Instead of large, greasy meals, tea room menus emphasized fresh ingredients and simple preparation.

However, you needed many skills to be successful at the tea room business. This is where Anna's education surely served her. Starting the tea room would have cost Anna around $500, in a day when her salary was likely less than that per year. Keeping the tea room records involved calculating profit and expenses, an important part of her success. Expenses such as employee wages, cooking ingredients, lantern fuel, and furnishings would have to be taken out of any profits.[35]

Anna had the advantage of not having rent to pay, having earned her homestead patent. But she had a good head for business, and was thrifty. With her profits, she began putting away money, not only for improvements to the Wigwam, but for future undertakings.

Just over the hill in the Tahosa Valley, a couple of miles south of the Wigwam, Charles Edwin Hewes, along with his brother Steve Hewes, and their mother Mary Kirkwood, the proprietors of the Hewes-Kirkwood Inn, were experiencing a different financial situation. The Hewes-Kirkwood resort provided lodging, meals and horseback rides to guests. Ever optimistic, and emboldened by rising guest counts and gross receipts, they made ambitious improvements to their establishment year after year, borrowing far more than they could afford to pay

back. After they defaulted on mortgage payments, loans for furnishings, and even loans from friends and relatives, Charles Edwin Hewes borrowed even more when he learned that a lumber company was going out of business, and he ordered 10,000 feet of lumber, and then shortly after that, purchased a 12-passenger automobile for $1100, putting $750 down. When things began to look grim and the prospect of losing their property loomed, Hewes sent a long letter about his financial woes to 200 of his regular summer guests, asking to borrow yet more money. Some of his loyal supporters stepped forward, and he obtained more loans to pay off his previous loans. Eventually, he defaulted on those, too.[36]

Anna's style was much different from Mr. Hewes'. She opened the Wigwam in 1914, and by 1920, she had earned and saved enough money to open a second gift shop on Elkhorn Avenue in the village of Estes Park, and called it "The Indian Shop." Eventually Anna changed the name of this store on Elkhorn to the "Whatnot Shop," probably to appeal to a wider array of customers.

The Hewes-Kirkwood Inn, which was about two miles south of the Wigwam, with the Estes Cone behind it.

Shortly after opening her downtown store, she had another business built at Beaver Point, at the location of the former Sundeck restaurant, now currently Bird & Jim. It was a grocery store and filling station that Anna called "Beaver Point Store and Confectionary." Nearby along Highway 66, Anna built cottages along the river, calling them "Belknap Cottages," with a gift shop on the premises called the "Louise Gift Shop." (Today these cottages are called "Skyline Cottages). Anna ran these businesses along with her niece Louise Wolfrom Belknap and Louise's husband Jack.

In my research, I have searched many places for more information about Anna's businesses in downtown Estes Park. She owned the building on

or an inheritance from her mother, who died in 1896, but it doesn't seem likely. Anna's father, Louis Wolfrom, was a saloon owner from Duluth, Minnesota. He and Anna's mother divorced in the mid- 1880s, and Louis married Matilda Warner in the early 1890s and had five more children. A saloon owner with a large family probably didn't have a lot of extra money to help out a daughter from his first marriage.

We know that Anna Wolfrom had a collection of Wedgewood China that she used at the Wigwam, because after she no longer operated the Wigwam as a tea room, Anna loaned the collection to the Dallas Museum of Fine Art. Upon her death, Anna's niece Louise inherited the collection, so the museum turned it over to her. Louise never had children,

The Wigwam sign.

Elkhorn (Estes Park's main street) where she operated a business from about 1920 to 1938, when she sold the building to Harriet Byerly, owner of the National Park Hotel next door. No photo of the Indian Shop seems to exist. It's frustrating that so little evidence of Anna's multiple Estes Park businesses has been preserved. It appears as if Anna's industriousness and success was dismissed or ignored, even though what she was doing was so unusual for a single woman at that time. Or perhaps the reason why it was ignored was because it was unusual.

Anna had managed to start her tea room with savings from her salary as a schoolteacher. It could be that she had help in the beginning from her father,

and after she died in 1966, it is unknown what happened to the collection.

I tried finding some evidence of what happened to Anna's china collection through Anna's living relatives. Unfortunately as time marches on, details are often lost forever, especially since neither Anna nor Louise had offspring. Anna's great half-nephew, Jak Wolfrom, was very helpful in providing more detail about Anna's life. He explained that his Aunt Joan (Anna's half- niece) lived with Louise in Phoenix after Louise was widowed. Since Joan stayed in the Phoenix house after Louise's death, she may have had possession of the Wedgewood China set. Sadly, Joan is in poor health and it's not possible to ask her. If I had only researched Anna's life a few years earlier, I might have been able to learn what happened to Anna's Wedgewood China, and other important facts about Anna's life.

We are all busy with our lives, and don't often think about how people living a century from now might want to know more detail about how we spend our days, what kind of tasks are necessary, and what's important to us. Likewise, Anna probably never gave a thought to people in the future who now would love to know a little more about what it was like running the Wigwam, or hear first-hand about her love for the Estes Park area. If it occurred to her, she would probably have taken the time to write about her experiences during those years, as she did when she was younger.

31. National Geographic Society https://nationalgeographic.org/news/woman-sufrage
32. Whitaker, Jan., *Tea at the Blue Lantern Inn: A Social History of the Tea Room Craze in America*, New York: St. Martin's Press, 2002.
33. Jack and Lulabeth Melton, *YMCA of the Rockies: Reflections, Traditions and Vision*, Estes Park, CO: YMCA of the Rockies, 2006.
34. https://www.tea.co.uk/the-history-of-the-tea-bag
35. ClickAmericana.com. *The Magic of Tea Rooms* (1905)
36. Pickering, James. In the *Vale of Elkanah: The Tahosa Valley World of Charles Edwin Hewes*. Estes Park, Colorado: Alpenaire Publishing, 2003.

5
CHAPTER

Whatnots in the Woods

Every seat was occupied at the tables on the open porch of the Wigwam. Amidst the conversations you could hear the tinkling of a spoon stirring sugar into a teacup, and the ice cubes clinking as a thirsty customer drained his iced tea glass. The air was fragrant with appetizing smells coming from the kitchen. Waitresses with cotton calico aprons over long skirts hurried between the kitchen and porch, carrying plates of ginger cake and cherry pie.

Many early tea rooms like the Wigwam popularized the tradition of eating outdoors.[37] It's easy to imagine why. While sitting on the Wigwam's porch, many years, and eventually Jessie managed the Indian Shop, the new business Anna started on Elkhorn in downtown Estes Park. The Wigwam became so popular that by 1917, Anna had employed four young women to assist her in running the business.

Jessie and Helen Smyth were valued employees for many years, and good friends of Anna's. Helen eventually married Miles Engelbach, and in 1926 made her home near the Wigwam in Webster's Big Horn Park subdivision, continuing the longstanding friendship with Anna. Helen and her sister Jessie were named as beneficiaries in Anna's will, each receiving a $1000 bond.

Many early tea rooms like the Wigwam popularized the tradition of eating outdoors. It's easy to imagine why. While sitting on the Wigwam's porch, Anna's customers could enjoy dramatic views, and be cooled by mountain breezes while enjoying their refreshments.

Anna's customers could enjoy dramatic views, and be cooled by mountain breezes while enjoying their refreshments.

The Wigwam became more and more popular. The increase in business required more help, and Anna hired two of her friends from Kansas City, the sisters Jessie and Helen Smyth, to assist her in the tea room. The Smyth sisters were teachers and colleagues of Anna's. They worked for Anna for

Anna had tapped into two very fashionable trends with her business, and her timing couldn't have been better. Railroad tourism to the West was exploding, and between 1890 and 1930, the Western market became very strong for Native American crafted objects such as basketry, rugs, and blankets. Anna made sure the Wigwam had a large inventory of Native American pottery, basketry, moccasins, beaded bags, and blankets. That, along with tasty

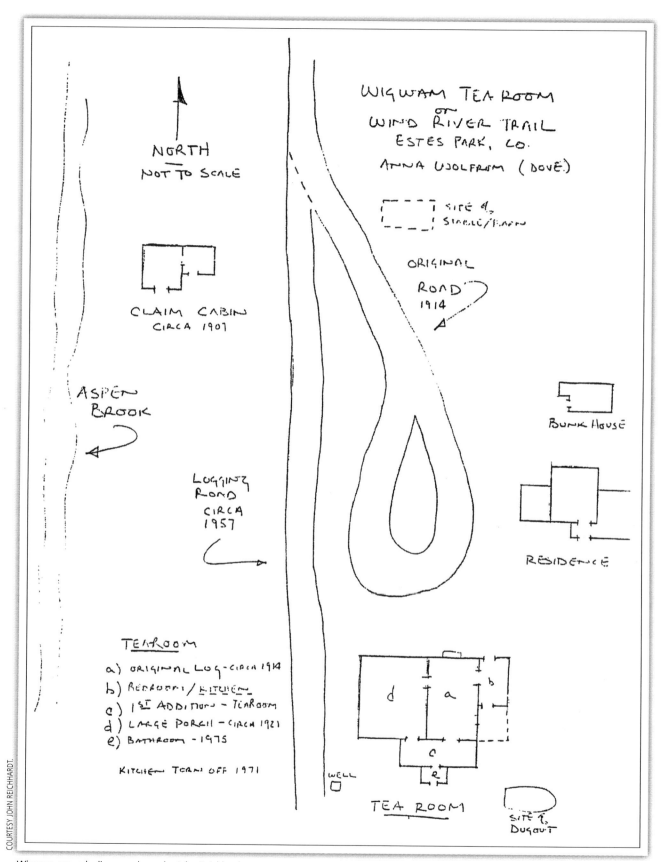

Wigwam grounds diagram, drawn by John Reichhardt.

beverages and foods served in an appealing, homey atmosphere, served by a woman with a winning personality, made for a very successful combination.

————◆————

As her business flourished, Anna built additional cabins on her homestead, one of which she made her home so that the tea room and curio shop could occupy all of the largest cabin. In 1918, she borrowed $900, likely to build her residence cabin, and/or to add the bunkhouse to house her staff. [38] In 1921, Anna added onto the Wigwam, doubling the size of her tea room, and making more room for the souvenir shop. [39] This tea room addition extended the west side of the building, and eliminated the stairs on the right side of the chimney that are shown in the earliest photographs of the Wigwam. This large addition was an open-air porch with generous openings on three sides overlooking a stream, a meadow of wildflowers, an aspen grove and pine forests, with a backdrop of the dramatic snow-capped Mummy Range.

Anna and her staff may have served small sandwiches, with the bread cut in the shapes of diamonds or circles, or tiny scalloped cakes, either frosted or dusted with sugar, still warm from the oven. They served candies, too, such as homemade caramels or fudge.

The location of the Wigwam became a happy accident for Anna. The Wind River Trail led hikers through a large aspen grove that opened into a meadow where Anna's cabins stood on a gently sloping hillside. Beyond the cabins as you looked south were gentle pine-covered hillsides with craggy granite outcroppings. This route was popular for hikers and horseback riders on their way to Longs Peak, or to destinations such as Lily Lake, Eugenia Mine, Estes Cone or Chasm Lake.

Isabel and Anne Pifer were sisters and guides at the YMCA. Their father was employed at the YMCA and involved in the Summer School Program. The Pifer family spent summers in the same cabin at

the Y for years starting in 1920, when the girls were teens. As Anne and Isabel hiked more and more in the mountains they loved, they began to lead other hikers, and became unofficial hike masters. People at the Y thought the girls were odd, since this was an unusual way for teenage girls to spend time in those days. Some hikes were lengthy ones and others were more leisurely, in the style Enos Mills was famous for, stopping to identify plants and flowers, encouraging people to take the time to maximize their experience of the natural world.

The sisters led hikes from the YMCA for four summers. Several times each summer they led hikes to the top of Longs Peak. They would assemble a group on the YMCA grounds at 3 or 4 a.m. and set out on the Wind River Trail to Highway 7, past the Wigwam and further south, passing Enos Mills' Longs Peak Inn at about sunrise. One sister took the lead and the other followed the last hiker. When the trail became strenuous, the girls sang songs to lift the group's spirits. [40]

On the way back, the hikers stopped at the Wigwam for rest and refreshments late in the day. Finally they would return to the YMCA grounds at around 7 or 8 p.m., and collapse into the bathhouse tubs. This route was about 26 miles round trip with an elevation gain of 6200 feet. By contrast, today's hikers who start out on the Longs Peak Trailhead several miles south of the old origination point hike 16 miles with an elevation gain of 4800 feet. [41]

————◆————

The Arapaho Indians camped near the shores of Mary's Lake near what would become the village of Estes Park during summers in the 1850s. The Ute and Apache traveled through, often fighting with the Arapaho. But the harsh winter weather likely dissuaded any tribe from attempting to survive the winters. Perhaps as a tribute to these earliest visitors, Estes Park became a popular place to purchase Native American jewelry, pottery, blankets, and artifacts. At one time, you would be hard-pressed

Two of Anna's published books of plays, *Human Wisps, Six One-Act Plays*, and *Albion and Rosamond and The Living Voice, Two Dramas*.

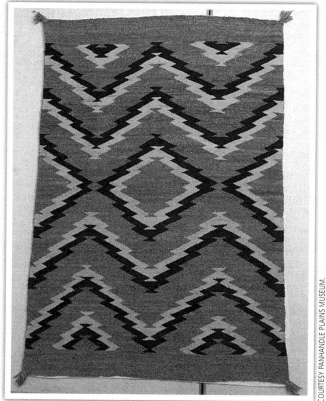

TOP: An Indian blanket from Anna's large collection, which she donated to the Panhandle Plains Museum in Canyon, Texas. BOTTOM: Indian pottery from Anna's large collection, which she donated to the Panhandle Plains Museum in Canyon, Texas.

to find any store in Estes Park that did not have even a small collection of Indian merchandise.

The plethora of Indian merchandise in Estes Park could also have been due to the fact that so many early shop owners, Anna included, spent time in the Southwest during the winter months, a natural place to acquire an impressive inventory of artifacts and art. After testing the market, shop owners realized that these things sold very well, and the trend in Estes Park grew.

The demand for these objects had to do with a social movement away from mass-produced, machine-made objects that had become commonplace because of the industrial revolution. Handmade items, which were considered more "virtuous and pure," were much trendier. This coincided too with the rise of the Arts and Crafts movement, and collecting Native American baskets, blankets, and beadwork became a fad. Collectors would set up special Indian rooms or corners in their homes to display their collections. Some people would buy hundreds of baskets during their travels.[42]

As a result, the curio shop became an important part of the business, and Anna, who by 1921 no longer taught school in the winters, began to spend winter months on buying trips to stock the souvenir shop. She purchased greeting cards and gifts, and Alaskan, Mexican, and American Indian pottery, rugs, dolls and other crafts. She also carried Philippine embroideries such as collar and cuff sets, belts, and bags, perfectly embroidered on the finest linens. [43]

Anna and her assistants also spent their spare time in winter months creating items by hand to sell in the curio shop. Some of the most sought after items were

The original Wigwam cabin, as it looked when it was first built. Lily Mountain stands behind it.

The Wigwam after Anna added on, extending the porch to serve more tea room customers. Note the Wigwam sign tacked to the tree on the right.

The Wigwam today, northeast corner. The open porch used to be Anna's kitchen, but later the kitchen was moved and this became an open porch for firewood storage, etc. Note the new roof.

The Wigwam today, northwest corner. You can see the faint markings where the stairs used to be, leading to the open porch where Anna served guests.

Anna's residence cabin as it looks today. After enjoying some years of success with the Wigwam, Anna built a separate residence for herself so her living space could be separate from her business. All of the Wigwam buildings are currently boarded up to protect them from vandalism and rodents.

The bunkhouse, where Anna housed employees who helped with her flourishing business.

nut bowls made out of red cedar and polished smooth on a turning lathe. The brilliant colors of the wood grains were "wildly extravagant in her color pallet, that the bit of red cedar becomes an emblem of the whole highly chromatic trip."[44] Selling the souvenirs became a profitable venture for Anna, as visitors were eager to take home something to remind them of an enchanting visit to a unique place.

Anna also sold books she had authored in her gift shop. They were among some of the best-selling items purchased by visitors at the Wigwam.[45]

During these winter buying trips Anna began her own collection of Native American goods, which eventually became very extensive. Exposure to these arts and crafts, and to the Native Americans themselves, caused Anna to develop a great interest in and respect for their culture. Before her death, Anna had the foresight to donate her large collection of Indian artifacts to the Panhandle Plains Museum in Canyon, Texas, where it remains today.

The Wigwam as it stands today is dramatically different from the photographs that have been preserved of it during the early years, mostly because of the largest addition of a porch built in 1921 on the west side of the building that replaced a smaller porch. Also, in later years, several large pine trees grew close to the building on two sides, so the view you see today of the north and west sides is partly obscured. But if you look for the old stone chimney, you can compare it to the original photos for orientation.

Anna's homestead eventually included four cabins and a stable. All but the stable are still standing as of this writing.

Anna's business was probably affected by the Great Depression. Business in Estes Park decreased,

By 1931, Anna was no longer operating the gift shop from the Wigwam and had moved that part of her business entirely to downtown Estes Park. She leased the Wigwam to Kansas City schoolteachers Lottie Reber and Margaret Taylor, who operated it as a tea room for at least two seasons. Lottie was a widow, and her children Barbara and John spent the summer at the Wigwam, too. [47]

Margaret Bangs and Lala Van Arsdale spent a treasured month with their teachers Ms. Reber and Miss Taylor at the Wigwam during the summer of 1932. In a letter addressed to Carol and Carl Reichhardt, subsequent owners of the Wigwam, many years later, Margaret describes her fond memories of her time at the Wigwam that summer. She remembers learning

---

The Wigwam as it stands today is dramatically different from the photographs that have been preserved of it during the early years, mostly because the largest addition of a porch built in 1921 on the west side of the building that replaced a smaller porch.

---

but the economy didn't suffer as dramatically as it did in most parts of the country. A likely reason is that Colorado became a destination for many tourists who could still afford to travel but could not afford more costly destinations during the Depression. Still, Estes Park did not enjoy the same numbers of tourists that it had before, and business owners had to find ways to cope. Many lodge owners were desperate for income during this time, and when Rocky Mountain National Park offered to buy their lodges in exchange for long term leases, many eagerly accepted the offers, which may have saved them from closure. This was a new strategy for the National Park Service, with the ultimate goal of eliminating man-made structures and bringing back an undisturbed, natural state.[46] Ultimately this policy would result in many well-loved historic structures being destroyed, a controversial practice.

the names of wildflowers, the mountain peaks, and hiking with a tin cup tied to her belt, while carrying a peanut butter and banana sandwich. They paid 10 cents for a weekly bath at the YMCA, since the Wigwam had no running water or electricity. She acknowledges that she was a very lucky girl for her parents to be able to afford the $100 it cost to stay a month at the Wigwam during the Depression. [48]

The *Estes Park Trail* describes the wildlife around the Wigwam in an article dated June 19, 1931. "The famous Rocky Mountain Big Horn sheep are found near the tea room and last year a mountain lion killed one of them just a quarter of a mile from the house. The cries of the sheep could be plainly heard." It also tells of a porcupine that lived under the Wigwam, until it was eaten by a bobcat. Other wildlife mentioned were gray timber wolves, and many deer, coyotes and bears.

Margaret Bangs, (right) and Lala Van Arsdale (left), standing on the south side of the Wigwam. They spent a month living there with their teachers the summer of 1932.

Anna operated the Wigwam successfully as a tea room for about 16 years. The trendiness of tea rooms and the increasing popularity of railroad tourism in the West helped create the success. Besides that, the unlikely yet convenient location Anna chose along Aspen Brook was the perfect location. Propelled by a strong work ethic, Anna created a very profitable business that ended up being the springboard to many other successful endeavors.

—◆—

Sadly, the recorded history of the years Anna operated the Wigwam tea room ends here. The details that have been preserved give us a glimpse into her fascinating life, but much is missing. If more importance had been placed years ago on preserving specifics about her unique history and life events, we would have a much richer story to tell. But the people who knew Anna have passed on, and those who appreciate her legacy are left to imagine the rest of her story.

However, the Wigwam itself was the setting for many events that took place after Anna's day, and what happened in the successive years is an important part of the story of this legendary cabin in the woods.

37. Whitaker, Jan., *Tea at the Blue Lantern Inn: A Social History of the Tea Room Craze in America*, New York: St. Martin's Press, 2002.

38. Mortgage Deed for $900 from the Estes Park Bank (abstract), March 18, 1918.

39. *Estes Park Trail*, October 7, 1921.

40. Jack & Lulabeth Melton, *YMCA of the Rockies: Spanning a Century*, YMCA of the Rockies, Estes Park, CO: 1992.

41. Robertson, Janet., *The Magnificent Mountain Women: Adventures in the Colorado Rockies*, Lincoln, NE: University of Nebraska Press, 1990.

42. Marks, Ben. "How Railroad Tourism Created the Craze for Traditional Native American Baskets," *Collectors Weekly*, July 1, 2014.

43. Estes Park Trail, September 5, 1914.

44. "A Woman's Tea House in the Wilderness," *Kansas City Star*, June, 1916.

45. "Woman Builds Mountain Home With Own Hands," St. Louis Post-Dispatch, July 1917.

46. Sommer, Jenny, Crowley, Elizabeth & Griep, Karen, *History of the Lodges of Estes Park & The Irrepressible Women of Estes Park & Their Lodging Establishments*, Estes Park, CO: Published by Warren Clinton, Castle Mountain Lodge, 2015.

47. *Estes Park Trail*, June 19, 1931.

48. Bangs, Margaret, Letter to Carl & Carol Reichhardt dated January 3, 1984. Courtesy John Reichhardt.

6
CHAPTER

Anna's Roots

One summer in the mid-1890s, Anna posed with her family for a photo in front of their home in Duluth, Minnesota. Her father Louis, her stepmother Matilda, and she and her siblings looked somber. Her body language as she stood in the back shows how out of place she felt next to her father's brood, her younger half-siblings Louis, Clara and Mary. She didn't really know them, having lived with her mother in Kansas City since her parents' divorce when she was about eight. Yet she must have been comforted by the presence of her brothers Philip and James. She adored Philip, and she rarely got to see her brothers at this point in her life.

The Wolfrom family, posing for a portrait outside their Duluth, Minnesota home. Left to right: Anna's brother Philip, Anna's sister-in-law Anna, Anna's brother James, Anna's half sister Mary (seated), Anna (standing), Anna's half-brother Louis Jr., Anna's half-sister Clara, Anna's father Louis Sr., and Anna's stepmother Matilda.

Art students sketching zoo animals at the Menagerie du Jardin des Plantes, a Paris zoo. Philip spent a lot of time here, doing exactly this.

Anna's mother died in 1896, perhaps not long before this photo was taken. With her brother Philip out West, and the rest of the family in Minnesota, Anna and her mother were companions and house-mates in Kansas City. It's likely that Anna's life was turned upside down after her mother's passing, and could be the reason she spent time with the rest of the family in Duluth that year.

Anna's parents were Louis A. Wolfrom (1845-1922) and Anne Rankin Wolfrom (1842-1896). Louis and Anne had four children: James R., born in 1866, Frank, born in 1867, Philip H. born in 1870, and Anne (Anna), born in 1872.

About the time Anna was eight years old, the family moved to Kansas City, Missouri from Duluth, Minnesota. The census for 1880 lists Louis, Anne, and children James, Philip and Anna, so Frank probably died prior to 1880, when Anna

was a young child. Louis' occupation was listed as barkeeper.

Anna's parents divorced sometime between 1880 and 1884. At that time, Louis moved back to Duluth and left Anne and the children in Kansas City.

Anna's brother Philip was an important part of her life. A handsome man with a kind face, he shared Anna's love of nature. At age 18, he left the family home in Kansas City. He was drawn to the open spaces of the Western frontier, where he had jobs herding cattle on horseback in Colorado, Arizona and Texas. This left Anna, two years younger than Philip, and her mother as the sole family members in their Kansas City household. The Kansas City directory of 1889-1891 lists Annie Wolfrom, teacher, and Annie Wolfrom, widow of Louis, living in one household. This indicates that Anna taught school beginning at just 18 or19 years old. This also demonstrates that Anna's mother posed as a widow,

Anna Wolfrom.

Philip Wolfrom, Anna's beloved brother.

a common practice because divorce was stigmatized in that era.

During his time in the West, Philip became an excellent horseman and had a quick and accurate toss with a lasso. He loved the wide open spaces of the West, but he also loved intellectual pursuits and spent much of his time studying, by some accounts even while in the saddle. He also began to nurture his artistic talent, sketching steers and horses in his free time.

Eventually Philip's love of learning led him back East. He had read about places he wanted to explore, and things he wanted to learn. Philip spent his time in New York museums studying art and in libraries studying books, eventually enrolling in the Art Students League of New York. He was fascinated by animals, and when in art school in Paris, he spent a lot of time sketching animals in the Menagerie du Jardin des Plantes, a zoo that is part of a large botanical garden in Paris. He also became known for his renderings of broncos and steers which he had become familiar with on the Western front, and later for his sculptures of animals. Philip's renderings of zoo animals eventually hung on the walls of the Wigwam, adding to its unusual and appealing décor.

A Central Park policeman noticed Philip, a tanned and assured rider, at ease in the saddle and demonstrating a lot of finesse while handling a horse. He offered Philip a position teaching riding to New York's police. This job sustained Philip while he pursued his studies.

Philip's early sketches were noted in art circles as being "clever," and his instructors at the Art Students League urged him to go to Paris to study art more seriously. The New York school provided a good starting point for Philip, but since the school offered no degree program or grades, it was a very informal atmosphere. Fueled by his early success, he left for Paris with very little money; his only assets were a stack of letters of introduction.

He began studies in 1895 in the Latin Quarter of Paris, studying at the Julian Academy, and later at the School of Beaux-Arts. Philip also perfected his painting and sculpture skills in the workshop studios of noted French artists Gerome, Fremiet, and Dampt, learning their techniques.[49] Some accounts have estimated that Philip studied art for a total of 12 years.

Anna visited Philip in Paris in 1895 and, inspired by Philip's European life, applied to the Sorbonne to study French Literature. She was very interested in becoming a writer. As an early testament to Anna's intelligence, she and one other American woman were selected for admission from among 100 American applicants. Anna joined Philip in Paris, and completed three years of study, from 1897-1899. In those years, brother and sister became very close. Their mother died in 1896, just prior to Anna's departure for Europe, when Anna was 24 years old. Their brother Jim lived in Duluth, far from the places Anna frequented. It's easy to see why Anna and Phil became so close. They had no other family members nearby, and their father had remarried and started a new family. Anna's diary mentions fond memories of times spent with Philip in Paris, dining near The Paris Opera and at Maxim's, and leisurely strolls down the Grands Boulevards.

He had been her companion, playmate and fellow student for years. They were a team with a special bond who had great adventures together, far away from and separate from the rest of the family.

As soon as she felt he had recovered enough to travel, they departed for the United States on the steamship Rotterdam. Unfortunately, Philip had not recovered at all.

In an outburst, he assaulted a nurse and broke a window attempting to escape from the ship's infirmary on the third day of the voyage. Part of Philip's anguish was that he had fallen in love with a beautiful art student in Paris, Anetta Trasor. But Anetta shunned his affections, despite his persistence,

---

Anna's studies at the Sorbonne were interrupted in order to take Philip back home to the United States. After arriving in New York, she arranged for his care and visited him regularly at Bellevue Hospital.

Philip became well known as an artist and sculptor, and is listed in "Who Was Who in American Art." He originally went to Paris to study painting and drawing, but sculpture became his specialty. Some of his sketches are still owned today by the Brooklyn Museum of Art and by the Panhandle Plains Museum in Canyon, Texas. One article described a masterpiece Philip had sculpted, an elephant that the Academy of Design displayed in 1901.

Anna and Philip's Paris life ended abruptly in March of 1899 when Philip developed a mental illness so severe that he had to be hospitalized. Determined to escape, he stole away from the hospital through a second story window late one night. Police finally captured the crazed man at 4 a.m., and returned him to the mental hospital.[50]

Anna was devastated by Philip's condition.

because of her dedication to her art. Philip still held out hope that one day they would be together, even crying out Anetta's name across the water as the Rotterdam pulled away from the shores of France.

St. Louis and New York newspapers told of the sad saga. Philip had to be placed in a straightjacket for the remainder of the voyage back to New York.[51] Anna's studies at the Sorbonne were interrupted in order to take Philip back home to the United States. After arriving in New York, she arranged for his care and visited him regularly at Bellevue Hospital. Their father, Louis, stayed in Duluth with his family. By this time, he had three young children and a new wife to care for. Anna undoubtedly missed her mother very much during this difficult time.

Anna's diary describes her commitment to take responsibility for Philip both emotionally and financially:

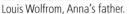
Louis Wolfrom, Anna's father.

James Wolfrom, Anna's brother, and father of Louise.

Louise Wolfrom Belknap, Anna's beloved niece.

"Went to Central Islip to see Philip. Found that he had grown very fleshy. He was smiling and waiting for me. In his delusions he never forgot Anna. He always said with such tenderness, 'You will never desert me, will you Anna?' It seemed he must have realized his state of dependency."

Frequent travel and schooling overseas had to be expensive. Perhaps the reason Philip and Anna could afford to be educated in Europe was that they inherited money from her mother's side of the family. Anna's living relatives have described the reason Louis divorced Anna's mother was because she was "snooty." But Anna's diary offers no clue about how she afforded her Sorbonne and Oxford schooling, or her lengthy trips to Ireland, Norway, Sweden, and Denmark. Her diary mentions her commitment to support Philip, which also suggests that her family had no extra money to help her, deepening the mystery.

Eventually Philip recovered enough to be released from Bellevue Hospital, and he spent two years gaining his health back, likely staying with family. The summers he spent in Duluth, and the winters in Kansas City. Then in 1901, he returned to New York to resume his art career, opening a studio where he worked every day. One day he left the studio for lunch, and upon his return he discovered the studio engulfed in flames. The fire department had just arrived, and prevented him from entering to save some of his work. All the work Philip had produced and accumulated during a very productive period was destroyed.[52]

Philip's fragile mental state did not handle this loss well. Bystanders describe his reaction to the fire as a hysterical laugh. In the weeks following the fire, he repeatedly returned to his burned out studio and attempted to sleep there at night. The occupants who lived in the area complained to the police. So, the police arrested Philip for trespassing and once again, he was committed to Bellevue Hospital.[53]

During this time at Bellevue and then later when transferred to the State Mental Hospital at Islip, Anna stayed nearby and visited her brother regularly. She looked after his every need, and her diary also describes buying him new clothes. He still mentioned Anetta frequently, and held out hope that one day he would win her over. During that time, the *Duluth News-Tribune* described Anna as being a writer for a number of magazines.[54]

69

Philip died in the mental hospital at Long Island, New York in 1904 of paresis at just 34 years old. Had his mind not been clouded by such severe mental illness, he could have been one of America's most well-known artists. Anna describes his death in her diary, and her relief that Philip was finally at rest:

How peacefully he slept in his casket, how nice he looked! Death had smoothed out the weird lines that insanity brings. As rest from that wild, exacting brain that craved freedom. And I, too, rested.

Anna had lived on edge for years while caring for Philip. It's obvious from her diary that she felt the mental illness took him away from her years earlier, and that his death was a sad relief.

Philip's story wasn't the only tragic one in the

a teacher did not include earning a college degree, but Anna was probably required to take a test that certified her to teach school.

After moving back to Duluth, Louis operated a liquor store and bar. He met and married Matilda Warner between 1884 and 1887, when Anna was in her early teens. Louis and Matilda had five children: Louis W., Rosa, (who died at age 10 of typhoid and was buried in a mass grave), Edward (who died at age 3) Mary, and Clara. Jak Wolfrom, one of Anna's living relatives, described the grief that Matilda suffered after Edward had a horrific accident, when he'd been chasing a toy across the kitchen floor and fell into a vat of boiling water. She had several more children after this incident, trying to replace Edward. Matilda's grief continued, as she had three infant boys who died at birth, and two more who didn't survive beyond age 5.[55]

With no offspring of her own, Anna had many deep relationships with friends and eventually with some of her half-siblings.

Wolfrom family. Anna's family history was checkered with difficulties.

Anna's father Louis was born in Germany, and her mother Anne was born in Ireland. Louis immigrated to the United States when he was about 15 years old, and when he turned 19, he enlisted in the US Army, and was assigned to the Company U of the New Jersey 10th Infantry Regiment. He was later stationed at Wilmington, N.C., as a part of the Company G of the 16th New York Heavy Artillery.

The divorce of her parents had to be traumatic for Anna. She was still a child when her father left her mother. He moved back to Duluth, Minnesota, the original family home. She then saw very little of her father until she was well into adulthood.

Anna became a schoolteacher by age 18 or 19. Obviously, the qualifications required to become

Louis' second family and the distance between Duluth and Kansas City caused Anna and her father to be somewhat estranged for a number of years. In her diary, she describes a visit from her father in 1905 saying that "father and daughter are just beginning to know one another." She would have been 33 years old during that visit.

Anna's brother James married Anna Felt in 1897, and they lived in Duluth, Minnesota, the family stomping grounds. Like his father, James operated a saloon, located just two blocks from his father's establishment.

In 1900, James and his wife had a daughter named Anna Louise, whom they called Louise. In Anna's diary, she describes meeting her little niece Louise on a visit to Duluth in 1905, saying:

Wolfrom Family Tree

Anna's Half Siblings

Rosa Wolfrom
Died age 10

Louis W. Wolfrom
1888-1965

Laura Ingberg

Darrel Weber

Clara Wolfrom
1895-1936

Mary Wolfrom
1893-1993

Merwin Murray

Edward
Died age 3

Anna's Half Nieces & Nephews

Margaret (Maggie)

Allan H
1922-2004

James Philip
1924-2014

Louis
1925-2010

Aileen
1927-

Joan
1930-

Sons Gordon, William & Douglas

Anna's Parents

Matilda Warner
1866-1944
2nd Marriage

Louis Wolfrom
1845-1922
Born in Germany

Anne Rankin
1842-1890
Born in Ireland

Anna's Siblings & Spouses

Anna S. Felt

James R. Wolfrom
1867-1954

Frank Wolfrom
1868-1880

Philip R. Wolfrom
1870-1904

Anna Wolfrom Dove
1872-1950

Orville Holmes Dove
1868-1948

Anna's Niece & Spouse

Anna Louise Wolfrom
1900-1966

Jack Belknap

No Children

"The hope of the dead comes back in the little niece. May she live to bless my fading days. Little Louise is the picture of me and my mother's only grandchild and sweet she is to living & dead."

Louise was the only offspring who was born to any of Anna's full siblings, so she was Anna's mother's only grandchild. Louise and Anna eventually became very close, when Louise moved to Estes Park and Anna took her under her wing. In Anna's later years, Louise undoubtedly looked after Anna, and their relationship became much like a mother and daughter. Louise eventually inherited most of Anna's estate.

Anna's older brother James also suffered from mental illness. He was hospitalized in Pueblo, Colorado, during the years when Anna lived in Estes Park. Fortunately, he recovered enough before the end of his life to spend time living near his daughter in Estes Park for a few years.

Neither Anna nor Philip ever had children. Their brother James had just one child, Louise, who bore no children, either. The direct descendants from the marriage between Anna's father and mother ended at Louise Wolfrom Belknap's death in 1966.

Anna's half-brother Louis W. Wolfrom (1888-1965) married Laura Ingberg, and they had five children: Allan H., James P., Louis, Aileen, and Joan. Anna's half-sister Mary Wolfrom married Merwin Murray, and they had three sons: Gordon, William and Douglas. There are many descendants alive today resulting from Anna's father Louis' second marriage to Matilda Warner Wolfrom and the generation that followed.

With no offspring of her own, Anna had many deep relationships with friends and eventually with some of her half-siblings. Anna's half-sister Mary Wolfrom Murray and her family were intimately involved in the running of Belknap Cottages, a business Louise and her husband started in partnership with Anna. However, the only Wolfrom relatives named as beneficiaries in Anna's will were her niece Louise, and her half-nephew, James Philip Wolfrom.

Anna listed many friends in her will, gifting them with $1,000 or $500. It's obvious that she put a lot of thought into whom she wanted to benefit. To include such a long list of people shows that she had a kind and generous heart.

49. "A Kansas City Boy in Paris," *Kansas City Star*, 4/25/1897.
50. "Duluth Artist Now in a Hospital at Paris," *Duluth News-Tribune*, 3/11/1899
51. "Insane on the Rotterdam," *New York Herald-Tribune*, 3/28/1899
52. "Duluthian Dies in an Asylum: Philip Wolfrom, Promising Artist, Succumbs to Paresis," *Duluth News-Tribune*, 6/30/1904.
53. "An Artist Sent to Bellevue," *The New York Times*, April 1, 1901.
54. "End May Be Near," *Duluth News-Tribune*, 8/23/1901.
55. Oral interview with Jak Wolfrom, 5/31/17.

7
CHAPTER

Academics and Authorship

Anna was enchanted with Oxford University. She describes Oxford in late August of 1904 as the "dearest place," and she chose to resume her college education there, now that she no longer had responsibility for Philip. After his illness interrupted her Paris education in 1899, she went to work as a writer and a teacher for several years, first living in New York to be near Philip and later when he improved, moving back to Kansas City to teach school.

After Philip's funeral in July of 1904, Anna and her close friend Kathryne Farming sailed for Ireland in early August. Her diary describes the landscape of Ireland:

> *"Passing the lake . . . we looked back and got a good bird's eye view of the pass, weaving down between the cliffs on either side. A poor sample of mountains compared to our Rockies, but a pleasant change to the ever-rolling of the ocean"*

After a few days in Ireland, they traveled to Liverpool and then to Oxford, England on the train. Oxford's beauty captivated Anna, and she describes being "spellbound" by the city while touring Oxford's colleges. Anna and Kathryne both enrolled.

Before Oxford's fall session started, she and Kathryne had plenty of free time to explore. Anna's diary describes their visits to the Gardens of Trinity,

Oxford University, which Anna described as "the dearest place."

Wadham, St. Johns, Magdalene, and Meadow of Christ Church. They went to Warwick and visited the Feudal Castle. When not exploring the city, Anna spent her time writing.

In October, she studied Shakespeare, Keats, and Greek Dramas at Oxford. During this time, she continued writing, working on her book *The Pine-God,* which she sent off to Macmillan just before Christmas.

On the day before Christmas, Anna was surprised to receive a wire from Guy LaCoste, to whom she had been introduced by her friend Frank Webster. Mr. LaCoste let Anna know of his impending arrival to England and invited her to dine at the Hotel Cecil on Christmas Day. Since she had already planned and shopped for an American holiday feast with her schoolmates, she invited LaCoste to join them. She asked him the reason for his visit to England, and he said simply, "To buy Estes Park."

LaCoste was determined to succeed. He explained to Anna that his partners had sent many letters to Lord Dunraven, offering to purchase the land he owned in Estes Park, but Dunraven never responded. So, LaCoste offered to travel to England in person to find Lord Dunraven and try to convince him to sell.

For two days, Anna and Kathryne entertained LaCoste, showing him the 22 colleges that made up the University of Oxford, as well as the city itself. Then LaCoste invited Anna to go with him to the House of Parliament, where he needed to deliver some papers to Lord Dunraven, a representative there. So Anna went along, excited to go inside the

"these hearts were filled with love and tenderness for the girl who, six years before, had battled the voice of the doctors and had taken the brother from their arms to sail the seas for America . . . I felt a grudge; I carried a stone in my pocket and was ready to thrust it at everyone in order to be avenged."

Obviously Anna struggled with visiting Paris so soon after Philip's untimely death.

After winter break, Anna continued her studies at Oxford, as well as her writing. Her friend Kathryne did not continue at Oxford, and sailed for America.

Finally, after many roadblocks, challenges, stops and starts, Anna graduated from the University of Missouri College of Arts & Sciences in the spring 1907. Within a few weeks, she decided to make Estes Park her home.

---

building for the first time, as she had always admired it. During that visit, Anna and LaCoste briefly met with Lord Dunraven, whom she described as "a tall man with tufts of reddish hair."

Later, LaCoste explained to Anna that when he asked Lord Dunraven why he had never replied to any letters offering to buy his holdings, he said that he had always dreamed of returning to the beauty of Estes Park and didn't want to part with that dream. But, he finally realized that returning was impossible after being appointed as a representative in Parliament.[56]

⬥

Anna and Kathryne spent their winter break in Paris, where her memories of Philip's heartbreaking illness reignited her grief. She visited several of her French friends, describing that:

Anna mentions her ambition to write two books, one about Paris life, and another on French history. She completed a manuscript called *French History Tales* in May and sent it off to a publisher, but they declined.

At the end of June that year, Anna said her "brain was tired and not wishing to return to America I decided on a trip to Norway and Sweden." After a few weeks of traveling on her own, she returned to Oxford and began working earnestly on *The Sun-Ghost* from July 22 to September 4 of 1905. Then in September, she returned to America for good, after having spent a year at Oxford.

Anna began substitute teaching at a high school in Kansas City, which she enjoyed. But she had a determination to finish her college degree. Her diary describes the summer of 1906 in Columbia, Missouri studying German and Italian Renaissance History, where "it was hot and I boiled, but I stuck it out." Then in the fall of 1906, she enrolled for her final year at the University of Missouri.

The following year stands out in Anna's life.

Finally, after many roadblocks, challenges, stops and starts, Anna graduated from the University of Missouri College of Arts & Sciences in the spring 1907. Within a few weeks, she decided to make Estes Park her home.

Anna's photo in the University of Missouri yearbook from 1907 shows her as she looked just weeks before she moved to Estes Park. She wore a lacy blouse with a high collar, and a dark jacket, along with her graduation cap. Her cheeks and chin were round, giving us a hint that her body was round too, the result of years of time spent at her desk writing, and in the classroom teaching, with little strenuous physical activity. The photograph of Anna that was taken later in her life on the porch of the Wigwam, after she had toiled several years on her homestead doing all the heavy lifting and scrubbing, shows a more chiseled face and a tall, lean body. Her expression there is one of deep satisfaction.

Anna had a passion for writing, and she wrote many books and plays in her lifetime. She loved having the quiet time to write, and describes "discovering herself" when spending hours alone writing at Oxford. A few years later, she adored the time she spent alone during quiet winters at the Wigwam, which gave her uninterrupted time to write. Some of the books she self-published and kept in trunks so that she could sell them to tourists in the curio shop.

She finally refined her craft after much practice, and her books began to sell very well. In 1917 her best seller proved to be *Human Wisps*, which was based on her actual experiences.[57]

Anna's Drama studies at Oxford inspired her to begin writing plays. Previously, she had written the novel *Romance of Wolf Hollow*, in 1902, her first attempt at a book-length project. *The Kansas City Journal* review on January 11, 1903 described it as "ungainly in the manner of workmanship." She honed her writing skills while studying Drama,

ANNA WOLFRUM
Duluth, Minn.

Anna's graduation picture from the University of Missouri. Note the misspelling of her last name.

and by 1921, she had completed three collections of plays, *Albion and Rosemond & The Living Voice* (Two Dramas, 1916), *Human Wisps* (Six one-act plays, 1917), and *Sacajawea, The Indian Princess* (1918). These plays are described in another newspaper article from the *Columbia Evening Missourian* on December 20, 1921, as being "characterized as among the best of the modern plays."

Anna's diary tells of her hard work on manuscripts, some of which were accepted for publication, others not. After writing *Sacajewea*, Anna became interested in writing more about Native Americans. She describes her work on a number of plays that explore the intricacies of religion in Native American life. "Everything they do has religious

Anna's Books & Plays

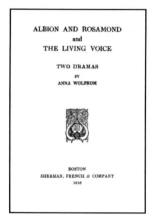  

Romance of Wolf Hollow, Gorham Press, Boston, 1902

The Pine-God, 1904, sent to Macmillan

French History Tales, May 1905, sent to a publisher, declined

The Sun-Ghost, Fall, 1905

Albion and Rosamond and The Living Voice,
Published by Sherman,
French & Company, Boston, 1916

Human Wisps, Six One-Act Plays, Sherman, French & Company, 1917

Sacajawea, The Indian Princess, 1918
Published by Burton Publishing Company
Kansas City, Missouri

significance. Their dance, their blankets, baskets, pottery and all have some relation to their religion."

If Anna authored additional plays after 1918, there is no record of them. The Reichhardt family, who later owned the Wigwam, discovered trunks full of unbound printed pages at the Wigwam when they acquired it in the 1950s, causing them to speculate that she self-published some of her books and printed large quantities to sell.[58] We know this is true because one of the articles about her in a Midwestern newspaper describes her books as one of the best-selling items in her curio shop.

56. "Account of the Purchase of Estes Park," *Estes Park Trail*, April 25, 1941 by Anna Wolfrom Dove.

57. "Woman Builds Mountain Home With Own Hands," *St. Louis Post-Dispatch*, July 1917.

58. Oral Interview with John Reichhardt, 3/14/17.

8
CHAPTER

The Women Get It Done

Tag sales. Bazaars. Dances. Card parties. Minstrel shows. Dinners and teas. These regular events were part of the social backbone of the village of Estes Park, but also and more importantly, raised the money for many essential services and improvements for the town. These fund raising events were the invention of the Estes Park Woman's Club, which was woven into every fiber of the life of early Estes Park.

Anna Wolfrom was a charter member of the Estes Park Woman's Club, which formed in 1912. The women of this club had an extraordinarily positive impact on the village of Estes Park, which as an unincorporated town, had no way of paying for the basic needs of a community. The Estes Park Woman's Club creatively and responsibly took on many projects that were essential to the village.

The Woman's Club Articles of Incorporation were filed on October 13, 1914, and signed by Mrs. William D. McPherson, Mrs. Eleanor Hondius, Miss Anna B. Wolfrom, Mrs. John D. Sherman, Mrs. Cornelius H. Bond, Mrs. Fred Clatworthy, and Mrs. James D. Stead.

The way the club formed was a testament to the spunk of these women. They had proven very effective at raising much needed funds for the various improvements of a fast growing tourist town. The Estes Park Protective and Improvement Association (EPPIA) struggled to raise funds after they organized in 1906, so they invited their wives and other women of the community to help them

Members of the Estes Park Woman's Club gather for a picnic at Stead's Ranch in 1913. Anna Wolfrom is missing from this photograph, but she was very involved with the club when this photo was taken, and many of these women were good friends to her.

raise money for projects. That was the beginning, and initially they called it the Ladies Auxiliary of the EPPIA.

The women organized events that raised considerable funds which they donated to the men. This went on for several years until the women decided to join forces with a new group that had formed called the Estes Park Businessmen's Association (EPBA). The two groups agreed to host dances every two weeks at various hotels as fundraisers. This money was mainly intended for roads and trails in the area.

The women had raised over $300 with all the events they had organized during the summer of

1912. That fall, Eleanor Hondius, treasurer of the EPPIA Ladies Auxiliary, brought the money to the EPPIA meeting, and suggested which trail and road projects the ladies considered the most important. However, the men told Eleanor that they appreciated the women having raised the money, but that since they were an Auxiliary, they could not dictate how the money would be used. Incensed, Eleanor left the meeting without turning the money over to the EPPIA.

Eleanor contacted several women who belonged to the Auxiliary and told them that the men would not allow the women's input on how the funds were to be used. As a result, the women decided to were still not treated as equals in society. The 19th Amendment to the U.S. Constitution, giving women the right to vote throughout the U.S., wasn't effective until 1920.

The Woman's Club contributions to the village of Estes Park were substantial. In the first year, they arranged for garbage disposal, and advocated and contributed toward the first tourist's bureau for visitors, organized a cleanup day and fed a hearty meal to all who helped. After Rocky Mountain National Park was officially formed, the club gifted a lot on Davis Hill to the Department of the Interior for a new administration building for the National Park.[59]

One of the first projects funded by the Woman's Club was a trail leading from the Elkhorn Lodge to the top of Deer Mountain. They also loaned $100 to a village committee for the purchase of a sprinkler cart to water Elkhorn Avenue, which regularly became extremely dusty with all of the carriage and horse traffic.

---

organize their own club for the advancement and improvement of Estes Park. They met for the first time on October 12, 1912, and initially named their club "The Ladies Improvement and Development Society," which they changed the following month to the "Estes Park Woman's Club."

One of the first projects funded by the Woman's Club was a trail leading from the Elkhorn Lodge to the top of Deer Mountain. They also loaned $100 to a village committee for the purchase of a sprinkler cart to water Elkhorn Avenue, which regularly became extremely dusty with all of the carriage and horse traffic.

The first year the Woman's Club formed, they earned over $1200 by hosting various fundraising events. These women must have felt proud and empowered to be so successful from the very beginning, independent of the men who had ordered them around, especially when women

Another of the earliest projects that the Woman's Club took charge of was the founding of a library. Initially they sought donations of books and magazines, and they borrowed books from the Colorado Traveling Library Commission. The first location for the library was the grade school, and it operated there from 1916 to 1920, with Mrs. Alma Bond as the librarian.[60]

After 1920, the library was housed in various locations. The Woman's Club rented a storeroom in Anna's building on Elkhorn where she operated the Indian Shop. Anna was paid $10 per month in rent. They charged a nickel for each book borrowed, and non-residents paid $1 for a library card.

The club planned to build a one-story log building to house the library and also space for club meetings and general entertainment, and in 1922, they had finally raised enough money to construct and furnish the building, which cost $5,000. The town

A group of civic-minded volunteers who spent the day gathering lichen rock for the front of the new Estes Park Library. Anna Wolfrom is seated at the bottom right foreground in the light dress, and to her right is Eleanor Hondius. Pieter Hondius Sr. is in the dark suit left of Anna, and Pieter Hondius, Jr. is standing next to his father.

The dedication ceremony of Rocky Mountain National Park on September 4, 1915. Second from left to right: Enos Mills, F.O. Stanley, Rep Edward Taylor, Mary King Sherman, and Colorado Governor George Carlson.

The Estes Park Library, which was founded by the Estes Park Woman's Club in 1920

donated the land in Bond Park. The club had enough funds on hand for a down payment of $3,500, and they borrowed the remaining $1,500. Within the first year, they had raised enough money to pay off the balance.[61]

The *Estes Park Trail* mentioned Anna as a frequent and generous contributor to the library fund in 1923, the year after the library opened, the same year she married Dr. Dove. A photo taken shortly after the library opened features Anna amongst a large group of people who had gathered to spend the day collecting rock that would be placed on the front of the new library. Anna is seated next to the Hondius family.

On September 4, 1915, the Estes Park Woman's Club supported the dedication ceremony of the new Rocky Mountain National Park by acting as hostesses for the event, which was held at the base of Horseshoe Falls, now the location of the Alluvial Fan, which was created by the Lawn Lake Flood. The women served hot coffee out of giant urns to adults and ice cream cones to the children.

One of Anna's fellow founding Women's Club members, Mary Belle King Sherman, gave one of the two keynote addresses to the audience gathered that day. Enos Mills, who worked so diligently to establish Rocky Mountain National Park that he is remembered as "The Father of Rocky Mountain National Park," gave the other keynote speech. Ms.

Sherman had worked tirelessly on the behalf of America's most scenic wilderness to establish the National Park Service. Her efforts were instrumental in the establishment of six of America's national parks.

Many members of the Estes Park Woman's Club were college educated. Wanting to keep their minds sharp, they often presented papers to one another to educate the group on topics each were knowledgeable about. Anna made presentations to the Woman's Club, once presenting the topic "One Act Dramas," a subject she had learned about from her study of drama at Oxford. She also presented the topic of "French Literature," based on what she had learned in her years as a student at the Sorbonne University in Paris. She also hosted another Woman's Club meeting at the Louise Gift Shop to show the club the collection of glassware she had obtained on a winter buying trip.

Anna Wolfrom participated as an active member of the Estes Park Woman's Club from 1912 until 1923, the year she married Dr. Orville Dove. Once married, Anna spent most of the year in Kansas City where Dr. Dove had a thriving medical practice, until he retired. Even after she was no longer a member, she continued to support the Woman's Club formation of the new library with generous donations.

59. Burgess, Harriet Rose, *Then the Women Took Over: A hundred Years of the Estes Park Woman's Club*, Estes Park, CO, Estes Park Museum Friends and Foundation, Inc. Press, 2012.

60. "Estes Park Woman's Club Has Operated Library 50 Years," *Estes Park Trail Vacation Edition*, March, 1966.

61. "Woman's Club Has Note Coming Due," *Estes Park Trail*, August 10, 1923.

9
CHAPTER

Businesswoman and Bride

It was a chilly January day when Anna, wrapped in a thick coat and scarf, took the arm of Dr. Orville Dove, as they made their way between bits of ice up the stairs leading to the Kansas City courthouse. Once inside, Anna's eyes shone as she removed her coat and scarf. She was dressed in her best outfit and had a new hat trimmed with lace. Arm in arm, Anna and Orville made their way down the corridor to the Justice of the Peace, exchanging smiles as they stopped in front of the entrance.

The *Estes Park Trail* mentions in their February 23, 1923 issue that "The many friends of Miss Anna Wolfrom, proprietor of the Wigwam Tea Room on the Wind River Trail, will be surprised to learn that she is to be married . . . She has been in Kansas City this winter teaching in the public schools, where she was employed before moving to Estes Park.

In letters received here she has announced her engagement to Dr. Dove . . . he has been practicing medicine in Kansas City 25 years. He and Miss Wolfrom will be married there . . . and come to Estes Park to make their home." Anna was 51 years old on her wedding date, an unusually accomplished first-time bride.

In the years preceding her marriage, Anna had displayed a talent for operating a profitable business, and with her earnings from the Wigwam, she expanded. After seven years of successfully operating the Wigwam Tea Room and Curio Shop, Anna opened a second location in the Village of Estes Park in 1920.

The Variety Store, Anna's shop in downtown Estes Park. Anna owned this building from 1920 to 1937, and during those years the store had several names, including The Indian Shop, The Indian Store, The What Not Shop, and the Variety Store.

The new store was located on the north side of Elkhorn Ave, just to the east of the National Park Hotel, which is now the Park Place Mall. The Estes Park Trail mentions that Jessie Smythe managed this shop for Anna, which left Anna time to look after the other businesses. She may have started out calling the store "The Indian Shop", but at some point she added or changed the name to "The Whatnot Shop," and then later to "The Variety Store." An ad from the Estes Park Trail on July 6, 1923 says, "Before buying those Indian Rugs, call at the Indian Store and What Not Shop, and see our exclusive line."

89

BEFORE BUYING

Those Indian Rugs

Call at the

INDIAN STORE

and WHAT NOT SHOP

And See Our Exclusive Line

Ad from the Estes Park Trail for Anna's Indian Store, June 15, 1923.

In 1920, Anna also established another business at Beaver Point (the intersection of Highway 36, High Drive and Mary's Lake Road—location of the former Sundeck Restaurant.) A photograph of the building advertises "Groceries" and "Root Beer," but an ad she placed in the Estes Park Trail calls it "Wolfrom Filling Station and Confectionary," selling Candies, Soft Drinks & Cigars." Anna had decided to use the reputation she earned at the Wigwam as an excellent baker to start a new business selling confectionaries in town. The folks who didn't have time to make it up to the Wigwam to savor her treats must have been happy to have easier access to the candies and cakes with such a mouth-watering reputation.

Downtown Estes Park from an overlook. Anna's store is dwarfed by the National Park Hotel next door.

Anna's Beaver Point Store, located at the intersection of Highway 36, Mary's Lake Road and High Drive. This is the location of the current-day restaurant Bird and Jim. High Drive is the road on the right, and Highway 36 is on the left.

The store also had a gas pump, which was one of the last chances motorists had to refuel before entering Rocky Mountain National Park. This business was very close to the cabin Anna eventually lived in at Belknap Cottages, making her daily commute easily walkable.

The building at Beaver Point became many different things during the years Anna owned it. We have evidence of the filling station and confectionary, but the photograph we have of the building shows it selling groceries and root beer, which the business could have evolved into. Vic Hoerner, longtime owner and operator of the Sundeck Restaurant at that location, reports that his family bought it in 1947, and at that time it was called the "Whistler Inn." Vic says that various entities operated it as a tea room multiple times before his family owned it, which opens the possibility that Anna could have operated an additional tea room at the Beaver Point location.

In 1931, Anna leased the building for three years to Buck Washburn, who opened Bucks Barbeque.[62] After Anna sold the building, it was operated as "Hap's Hamburgers," and in 1947, the Hoerner family bought the building and improved it, turning it into the Sundeck Restaurant. Over the years the family added onto the building six times.

Wolfrom Confectionery and Filling Station

CANDIES, SOFT DRINKS, CIGARS

That Good Volatile Texas Gasoline and Oils

AT BEAVER POINT

Ad from the Estes Park Trail for Anna's Wolfrom Confectionary, June 15, 1923

The Hoerner family operated the Sundeck in that location for 69 years, until Vic Hoerner sold it in 2016. Currently it is operated as the restaurant Bird and Jim.

Anna's niece, Louise Wolfrom Belknap, moved to Estes Park during the Wigwam years to join her Aunt Anna. Being single until age 51, Anna had no children of her own, and treated Louise like a daughter. Undoubtedly Anna had urged Louise to move to Estes Park, and when Louise and her husband Jack Belknap made the move, Anna took the Belknaps under her wing. In 1922, Anna purchased land on Highway 66 and financed the construction of another business called Belknap Cottages, which Louise and her husband Jack Belknap managed. Anna and Louise also ran a gift and antique shop

Current day photo of Anna's cabin in town at Skyline Cottages, formerly Belknap Cottages. Anna chose a delightful setting for her in-town residence just above the river and with a view of Longs Peak from her back porch.

called the Louise Gift Shop, on the grounds of Belknap cottages. The business today is called Skyline Cottages, located on Highway 66, just south of the junction of Highway 36 and 66.

Sue Lamb, current owner of Skyline Cottages, told me that Anna built one of the nicest cottages on the property for herself after she moved into town. Sue's manager gave me a tour of this cabin,

She built this cabin within a year of her marriage to Dr. Dove, so this is where they began their married life in Estes Park.

In 1944, crews completed the 13.1 mile Alva B. Adams Tunnel, which brought water through the Continental Divide from Lake Granby, Shadow Mountain Reservoir, and Grand Lake on the west side, under Rocky Mountain National Park, to the east side, where the tunnel ends near YMCA property on the west side of Highway 66. After this, the road was commonly referred to as "Tunnel Road," interchangeably with "Highway 66." From where the water comes out near Tunnel Road, it is released into Mary's Lake, Lake Estes, and is stored in Carter Lake, Flatiron Reservoir, Horsetooth Reservoir, and Boulder Reservoir for power generation and water use along the Colorado Front Range.[63]

In October 1949, less than a year before her death, Anna had the foresight to add Louise to the deed of the Belknap Cottages as a joint tenant, so that Louise would inherit the property free and clear. Anna died the following summer, and Louise became the sole owner of Belknap Cottages and the Louise Gift Shop. She continued to operate the

---

It's rare to find a place in Estes Park that has the advantage of both river frontage and mountain views, but Anna found it. She built this cabin within a year of her marriage to Dr. Dove, so this is where they began their married life in Estes Park.

---

which has been remodeled over the years but still has many of the original features. The location is unbeatable. It sits just above the melodious river and has an unobstructed view of Longs Peak, the tallest mountain in the area, from the back porch that also overlooks the river. It's rare to find a place in Estes Park that has the advantage of both river frontage and mountain views, but Anna found it.

cottages during the summers with her husband, Jack Belknap, until his death. Louise and Jack spent winters in Albuquerque, New Mexico for a few years and then had a home in Phoenix, Arizona near Camelback Road. According to Anna's living relatives, after Jack's death, other family members stepped in to help Louise. Mary Wolfrom (Anna's half-sister from her father's second marriage) helped Louise keep

Louise Belknap, Anna's niece, and Anna, on the porch of Louise's home in Phoenix, just off Camelback Road.

the cottages operating, and Mary's sons Gordon, William and Douglas Murray helped out too.

Louise sold the cottages in 1960. When Louise died, unfortunately Mary was too old by that time to return to Estes Park and claim any family memorabilia or valuables. Jak Wolfrom, a member of Anna's family, told me that because of this, important items that would tell us more about the history of Belknap Cottages were likely sold at a yard sale or thrown away.

In the years that Anna and Louise operated the cottages and gift shop on Highway 66, the road's character was very different than it is today. Between 1932 and 1960, an entrance to Rocky Mountain National Park, named the Thompson Entrance, was accessed about a mile south of Belknap Cottages, west of what is now the Dunraven Inn Restaurant on Highway 66. There the road traveled west from Highway 66 to the entrance station kiosk. Obviously, Anna was thinking of tourist traffic into Rocky Mountain National Park when she chose to locate three of her businesses on prime real estate along the main corridor entering Rocky Mountain National Park.

When the Thompson entrance station was first located there, the park did not charge admission. Beginning in 1932, they charged $1.00 admission per car for entrance into the national park. The Thompson Entrance existed as one of three main entrances into Rocky Mountain National Park until 1960, when park officials replaced it with the Beaver Meadows Entrance.[64]

The early 1920s were a busy time for Anna. The Wigwam's popularity was an established fact by this time, and even though Anna must have had her hands full with that, she chose to expand and open other businesses in town. After 1920, Anna's businesses in the Estes Park area included the Wigwam Tea Room and Curio Shop, the Shop/Whatnot Shop, the Beaver Point Store/Wolfrom Confectionary, Belknap Cottages, and the Louise Gift Shop.

By this time, Anna had met Dr. Orville Dove, a physician from Kansas City. She spent time in Kansas City during the winter months, and likely her friendship with Dr. Dove grew during these visits.

After her marriage, Anna spent winters with her new husband in Kansas City. When he retired and they were free to travel, they wintered in New Orleans and eventually established a home there. Never one to be idle, Anna opened yet another Indian Curio and Antique Shop in New Orleans, which she called "The Totem Pole." She also continued to operate the Shop on Elkhorn until she sold it to Harriet Byerly, who owned the National Park Hotel, in 1937.[65] The National Park Hotel expanded and built a bowling alley in the Indian Shop location.

By the mid-1930s, Dr. Dove's poor health forced him to live in a sanatorium near New Orleans. Anna corresponded with Harriet Byerly in 1948 about the sale of the property, which had once been "The Indian Shop" just east of the National Park Hotel, to Harriet. She mentioned in that letter that she was "stuck" in New Orleans because her husband was in a sanatorium there. Unable to get back to Estes Park, Anna must have longed to return. After a lengthy illness, Dr. Orville Dove died in 1948. After 25 years of marriage, Anna was single once again.

Anna was Orville Dove's third wife. He married Helen M. Black on October 15, 1901 when he was about 33 years old. Helen died in 1908[66], so Orville married a second time, this time to Florence Howard Peake, later that same year. Florence had a four-year-old son, George, from a previous marriage. Orville and Florence were married for at least 12 years, as the 1920 census lists them both, along with George, as living in the same household. But, apparently their marriage ended in divorce, because Florence lived until 1939. Orville Dove married Anna Wolfrom in 1923 when he was 55 years old. There is no indication of whether Dr. Dove continued to have contact with his stepson after his marriage to Anna.

In 1947, Anna began making plans to donate her extensive collection of Native American artifacts to a museum so that the public could enjoy it. She chose to donate it to the Panhandle Plains Museum in Canyon, Texas.

Why Canyon, Texas? In her letter to Dr. L.F. Sheffey of the Panhandle Plains Museum, she explained that she got into a conversation about Indian culture with some people who visited her Indian Store in Estes Park. She told them she was looking for a new home for her collection. Being from a nearby town, they suggested she look into the Panhandle Plains Museum because of Dr. Sheffey's interest in Indian lore.

Anna visited the Panhandle Plains Museum on May 20 of 1947 to meet with Dr. Sheffey and make a decision about donating her collection. Her train arrived in Amarillo at 10:15 p.m., and Dr. Sheffey gladly met her and escorted her to her place of lodging in Canyon.[67] Apparently she became satisfied that the Panhandle Plains Museum was a good home for her collection, as The *Amarillo Daily News* announced Anna's donation of 176 items on the front page of the paper on July 17, 1947. It describes the collection as "such objects as scalp locks, medicine brushes, game bags, headdresses, war clubs, bladder rattles, papoose cradles, leggings and the like. Nations represented are the Ojibways,

The Thompson Entrance to Rocky Mountain National Park (off Highway 66), which was the main entrance from the east side until 1960.

Sioux, Utes, Navajos, Omahas, Hopis and Winnebagos."

During the following two years, Anna donated many additional items from her Native American collection to the Panhandle Plains Museum. It was timely that she donated the last items in 1949, just a few months before her death. Some of the items that she also donated to this museum were drawings by her brother Philip Wolfrom, charcoal figure sketches that he completed while a student at the Beaux-Arts in Paris. The PP Museum today has a total of 248 items in the collection donated by Anna Wolfrom Dove.

Anna also donated several of Philip's sketches of zoo animals to the Brooklyn Museum before her death. Some of these were displayed on a gallery wall in the Wigwam during its years of operation.

At age 77, Anna thought she found love again. She married John T. McNamara in Kansas City, Missouri on May 13, 1949. The marriage quickly turned out to be a disappointment, and the following February, they separated. The marriage was annulled on March 8, 1950. Some have speculated that Anna found out Mr. McNamara was a gold digger and was simply after her money, since Anna had done well financially.

A letter Anna wrote to a friend on letterhead from the Hotel Imperial in Longmont dated June 1, 1950, mentions the annulment. In Anna's words "We are still the boy and girl sweethearts of forty years ago."

There is some longing in that statement, suggesting that their parting wasn't without regret. They had a long history, having known each other from younger days in Kansas City. Despite that, it appears likely that Anna discovered McNamara had turned out to be a different man than she remembered from so long ago. She prepared her last will and testament in September of 1949, just four months after their marriage, but all she bequeathed to McNamara was a thousand dollars cash.

That same letter mentions that she had been delayed in Longmont, where she was going through some testing at a clinic on her heart. She was hoping the tests would find her healthy enough to be able to return to Estes Park, which she referred to as "the Park," as was common then.

She did make it back to Estes Park, but her time there was cut short. A few weeks later, Anna died of Coronary Occlusion at the hospital in Longmont. Her niece Louise wrote to Anna's dear friend Kathryne Farming Boysen a few days afterward, informing her of Anna's sudden death. "It was such a shock even though I knew her heart condition was such that it could happen at any time. I feel so badly because she was unhappy these past few months. Her marriage was such a disappointment and was annulled last winter."

Louise's letter goes on to say that Anna had returned to Estes Park but was suffering also from arthritis in her back. On the morning of July 12th, Anna called a friend and asked to be taken to the Longmont hospital as she had been in so much pain the night before. After reaching the hospital and being examined by the doctor, she died in her sleep.

———◆◆———

Anna's death marks the end of her story, but the Wigwam Tea Room still stands, and has a rich history following the years Anna was alive. The Wigwam was and still is a legendary, cherished place for many who lived or visited there.

62. Reichhardt, John: Oral history of Program presented 11/21/1996, Estes Park Museum.
63. Wikipedia, *Alva B. Adams Tunnel.*
64. Rocky Mountain National Park Archives, "Historic Structures Part II," Ferrell Adkins Collection, Series #02.06 File Unit 033.
65. Pickering, James H., *America's Switzerland: Estes Park and Rocky Mountain National Park, the Growth Years*, Boulder, CO: University Press of Colorado, 2005.
66. Ancestry.com
67. Panhandle Plains Museum, Canyon, TX, correspondence file on Anna Wolfrom Dove.

10
CHAPTER

The Reichhardt Years

One bright morning, Carl Reichhardt stood at the Majestic stove in the cheery Wigwam kitchen, opened the fire box door and stoked the fire with a long poker. Bacon sizzled in a cast iron pan on top of the Majestic, creating a mouth-watering aroma. His wife Carol sat at the table, sipping a steaming stoneware mug of coffee, which Carl had just brewed in a big enamel coffee pot. After breakfast, he had big plans for a day of mixing mortar and re-chinking the logs that formed the Wigwam walls.

Sunlight streamed into the Wigwam kitchen through the window panes, and lit up a section of

160 acres to Earl Cogburn, Lawrence Cogburn and Thomas Redman in 1948. Anna financed the sale, but after her death, the buyers defaulted on the loan. So in 1953, Louise Wolfrom Belknap, Anna's niece and primary heir, repossessed the property because of the delinquent payments. In 1956, Louise sold the property for $15,000 to Carl Reichhardt, R.M. Markus, and Henry F. Markus. Two of those partners held it for 33 years.

Henry Markus worked for Carl Reichhardt as a bookkeeper, and R.M. Markus was Henry's uncle. When Markus and Reichhardt became interested in purchasing the property, Markus brought his uncle

---

In 1956, Louise sold the property for $15,000 to Carl Reichhardt, R.M. Markus, and Henry F. Markus. Two of those partners held it for 33 years.

---

the floor that was covered by a multicolored rag rug. Two wicker chairs beckoned from beside the stove. An armoire served as a pantry, and next to it was a vintage refrigerator, both painted a bright rusty red. The combination of the quaint furnishings, kerosene lanterns and colorful accents made the room a welcoming place.

Anna Wolfrom Dove sold her homestead property that included the Wigwam buildings and

in, primarily as an investor. The Reichhardt and younger Markus families planned to use the property, and agreed that the residence cabin (the smaller, newer cabin to the north of the Wigwam), would be for the Markus family to use, and the larger, older cabin, which had been operated as the Wigwam, would be used by the Reichhardt family.

The Markus family began by cleaning and furnishing the residence cabin, and building a new outhouse, but after a short initial time period, they

Carol and Carol Reichhardt at the Wigwam. The Reichhardts owned the Wigwam property along with two partners from 1956 to 1989. They sold the acreage for inclusion into Rocky Mountain National Park.

rarely used the property. Carl and Carol Reichhardt and their family, who lived in Greeley at the time, began to make improvements to their Wigwam cabin.

Carl worked as a Liturgical artist, designing and creating religious art for churches. He used handblown stained glass, bronze, wrought iron, and wood to make altars, crosses, stained glass windows, and various sanctuary appointments. He was successful and well-known at his craft, and his creations are in many churches throughout the United States.

Reichhardt and his partners did not have the same goals for the use of the Wigwam property. The Markus families had purchased the property primarily as a financial investment, and the Reichhardts wanted to use and preserve the property. Tensions rose because of these differing viewpoints, which could have been why the Markus family rarely used their cabin.

In the beginning, the three partners allowed Otis Whiteside of Estes Park to lease the land for logging, in order to offset the cost of purchasing the property. Unfortunately, the consequence of the logging resulted in an extensive tearing up of the land. Whiteside built logging roads and loading platforms throughout the 160 acres, primarily nearby the cabins. Meadows were dug up and ugly piles of slash were stacked everywhere for years. The one benefit that came from the logging was the road from the Wigwam to the south end of the property proved useful, as well as the road to the north toward Windcliff, which was and still is used as a hiking trail for many. After this, Carl Reichhardt's desire to preserve the land grew, and he refused to consider any of the Markus' proposals for selling off portions of the property for development.

Just north of the Wigwam on the hillside perched the rapidly expanding development called Windcliff Estates, developed by Don and Wylene Buser. The Busers had carved roads into the side of the mountain for their development below Teddy's Teeth, an unwelcome sign of progress to the families who lived along Aspen Brook and the Wind River Trail, who had enjoyed such unspoiled wilderness for many years.

Carl steadily improved the Wigwam. He worked on re-chinking the logs, replacing the roof, and restoring and repairing the building, recruiting help from family members whenever he could. The main level was in such bad shape at first that he ignored it, and began by finishing the lower level under the porch into a living space. He created a bedroom, storage room, and kitchen/living area with a wood stove. The west wall had large windows with a view of Aspen Brook and large blue spruce trees. At first, the family used an old propane stove for cooking, but eventually learned how to operate the Majestic stove that was left from the tea room days, which was superior in many ways.

In the early years, the family was absorbed with life in Greeley, and they rarely used the Wigwam while the children were school-aged. As they became older, that changed. In 1971, the Reichhardt family began spending weekends restoring the main level, which they hadn't used for the first 15 years. They tore out the old unstable kitchen that had been an addition on the east side of the building, making it into a covered shed/entry, and built a new kitchen on the sunny south interior of the cabin. They had a goal for all of these renovations. After many weekends of preparation and hard work, the Reichhardt's son John and Ann Peddycord were married at the Wigwam in June of 1971.

The new kitchen, formerly a sunroom in Anna's day, was a warm, inviting room. A block of ice in the icebox kept their food cold, just like in the old days. Anna's sturdy Majestic stove was the heart of the kitchen. Carol regularly cooked on the old stove, making Midwestern Chili, German Potato Salad, or an old family recipe of Green Bean Soup. She prepared a lot of their meals ahead of time in her Greeley kitchen as well, and always brought along tins of homemade ginger and oatmeal cookies. Carl was usually the cook at breakfast time, mostly making bacon, eggs, toast and strong "Cowboy Coffee," which they all drank black.

Carol shopped regularly at second-hand stores in Greeley until she found items with the right amount of rustic for furnishing the historic cabin. She equipped the kitchen with handmade pottery mugs, stoneware, matching dinner plates, rag rugs and red ruffled curtains that matched the rusty red dining chairs. Even the shade on the kitchen kerosene lamp was red.

With the main level improved, the Wigwam had plenty of room for everyone. A large stone fireplace on the north side of the large living room provided warmth. The family furnished the living room with three big sofas to surround the fireplace, and a large coffee table for game playing. A large red painting by Ann Reichhardt hung on the living room wall, coordinating with an oriental area rug Carol bought for the floor. Carol also found unusual woolen quilts made out of old suits to use as bedspreads.

COURTESY JOHN REICHHARDT.

The logging road at the Wigwam.

COURTESY JOHN REICHHARDT.

The Wigwam west exterior wall in the Reichhardt years. The upper level has removable shutters closing the space, which were removed during summer months to make an open air porch. The lower level housed living quarters for the Reichhardts the first 15 years they owned the property.

The interior of the Wigwam porch, which illustrates how the removable shutters operated.

The oversized porch, where tea room customers were once served, was furnished with a set of twin beds, a long picnic table, and iron patio furniture from Mexico. Carol kept many bird feeders hanging from the porch, attracting hummingbirds and many other bird species. The many friends and family who visited were charmed with the setting, just as visitors had been in days gone by. After the family restored the cabin, they started using it most weekends, having fallen in love with what they called the "100 Acre Woods."

The wood coverings for the windows of the open porch were very large and cumbersome. Carl cut them in half and installed hinges on each side to make them into useable shutters. He also eventually installed windows on each side of the porch to let light in so it could be closed up and usable in cold weather. Carl always had a task for the family who visited, especially the men, either cutting down dead trees for firewood or shoring up the Wigwam foundation. The 1954 pickup Carl drove often got stuck in various locations on the property, and the men were always digging it out from somewhere.[68]

The family had a tradition of cutting the annual Christmas tree on the property. It had been enough years since the logging took place for many trees to grow into the perfect size for an indoor tree. The family brought home a beautiful Blue Spruce to their home in Greeley each year.

Carol & Carl's son John Reichhardt has fond memories of spending many a summer day at the Wigwam while growing up. "Working" on the claim cabin was a favorite pastime for John and other Reichhardt boys. With hammer, nails and old rusty saws, they tried to reattach siding or patch the deteriorating roof. The tradition continued for more than one generation of boys in the Reichhardt family, when John's sons spent time at the Wigwam with their grandparents.

When Louise Wolfrom Belknap sold the property to the partners, she told them that there were a couple of mine starts high on the hillside above the Wigwam. It took the Reichhardts years to locate them, but they finally found them, one a deep pit described by John Reichhardt as probably being on National Forest land. The other one had a more horizontal opening, on Wigwam property, up the hill from the southern end of the logging road that leads away from the Wigwam. Both are east of the Wigwam buildings on the hillside. The Reichhardts and others have speculated that these mine starts were probably created by Jimmy Fields, who may have continued to prospect even after filing his homestead claim.

Carl was a fun grandpa, and on many occasions he secretly planted shiny bronze filings from his work as a Liturgical Artist at the mouth of the horizontal mine above the Wigwam. He took many Reichhardt children and grandchildren up there to "mine" for gold, and they would be thrilled to find and collect their "riches."

The Reichhardt family had many a summer party at the Wigwam. Over the years, they hosted birthday and anniversary celebrations, and visits from friends and family. The Reichhardts had strong connections with their neighbors who lived along Aspen Brook, often having them over for meals and games. Spending time at the Wigwam grew into a treasured family tradition, and many of the Reichhardt's friends grew fond of the place, too.

The pathway and entrance to the Wigwam, by Judy Meyers.

The back porch of the Wigwam, by Judy Meyers.

Judith and George Meyers were friends of the Reichhardts from Greeley who visited the Wigwam often. Judith was an art teacher for the Greeley-Evans school district, and a well-known artist in the area. She was inspired to draw several sketches of the Wigwam, and she gifted those sketches to the Reichhardts.

Another artist friend, Dennis Reinke, painted a watercolor print of the entrance to the Wigwam and gave it to the family. They donated the Reinke painting to the Rocky Mountain Nature Association several years ago, and it still hangs in their offices, now the Rocky Mountain Conservancy.

In the early 1970s, Carl's son Fritz, an engineer, designed a system to bring water from a spring on the hill above the Wigwam down to the building. Soon thereafter, the family worked together to add a bath with a shower and toilet on the south side of the cabin. The only way to heat water for bathing

was in a sidearm reservoir on the Majestic stove, so showers were infrequent, but finally having indoor plumbing was a big improvement.

In 1972, Karen Reichhardt, Carol and Carl's daughter, found an old wheelbarrow at Jimmy Fields' cabin, next to the meadow just south of the Reichhardt property. At that time Jimmy's shack was still standing. The glass from the windows was long gone, and it had become just a shell of weathered wood. The remains of the shack can be found today on the northeast edge of the meadow north of the Wigwam, near the hitch rack.

Karen remembers camping there occasionally and noticing that Jimmy Fields had chosen the site for his cabin very strategically, because the morning sun bathed the site in warmth first, before anywhere else near the meadow. Karen brought the wheelbarrow back to the Wigwam. I asked her if she thought it was possible that it could be the same wheelbarrow

PHOTO BY AUTHOR, COURTESY OF THE ROCKY MOUNTAIN CONSERVANCY.

The Wigwam entrance, watercolor by Dennis Reinke

Jimmy used to haul Anna's supplies to the Wigwam before they completed the road all the way to the Wigwam. She thought it was entirely possible.

Several Reichhardt family members used the Wigwam as a temporary home on more than one occasion.

In 1974-75, Karen Reichhardt lived at the Wigwam for a year between college graduation and starting a master's degree program. She had taken a month-long wilderness class in college, and considered living full-time at the Wigwam to be an extension of that experience. Karen relished her time in nature at the Wigwam, hiking the property and nearby destinations frequently, and studying the flora and fauna, noting the frequent changes in plants as the seasons progressed.

Karen worked part-time at Outdoor World in downtown Estes Park, and also chopped wood for extra money. She baked whole wheat bread once a week on the old Majestic, which was difficult to get exactly right, as you couldn't tell what temperature the oven was. Chocolate chip cookies were less tricky, and she turned out batches of them beautifully.

Karen's friend and college roommate, Sarah Sullivan, joined her at the Wigwam for part of that year, and Rob, Butch and Sara Stockover, Karen's nephews and niece from Fort Collins, spent many weekends there too. Karen remembers wearing a coat indoors all the time during the winter, and

The wheelbarrow found by Karen Reichhardt at Jimmy Fields' cabin.

Jimmy Fields' cabin. Jimmy was Anna's closest neighbor, and a friend who helped her with many of the projects at the Wigwam.

sleeping inside two sleeping bags during a cold spell when temps reached 15 degrees below. She and Sarah snuck into the YMCA once a week for showers.

Sarah remembers her time at the Wigwam fondly, and didn't mind that it had no plumbing or electricity. She appreciated the warm fireplace and

Gouache painting by Sarah Sullivan, who lived at the Wigwam for a few months with Karen Reichhardt in the 1970s. Sarah painted this on a recent visit to the Wigwam.

What remains today of Jimmy Fields' cabin.

The barn/storage shed structure at the Wigwam, the only building from Anna's day that is no longer standing. The wood from the siding of this building covers the walls of the Notchtop restaurant in Estes Park today.

Majestic stove, and remembers there being a lovely place to sit and eat in the kitchen, and having a snug and warm place to sleep. Sarah is an artist, and she sketched many scenes around the Wigwam while living there. She recently returned to Estes Park and went looking for the Wigwam. It took some effort because it had been so long, but she finally located it. During her time there she was inspired to create a gouache painting of the Wigwam. As she did back in the day, she appreciates Anna Wolfrom for being gutsy enough to homestead alone, and she often felt Anna's presence during her time at the Wigwam.

Karen lived alone at the Wigwam for part of the year, except for the occasional weekend when her parents or nephews would come. Anna was often in her thoughts. Carl and Carol made the trip from their home in Greeley and spent most weekends at the Wigwam when the weather was nice, but less often in the winter.

Many of their neighbors along Aspen Brook Road had paid to bring in electricity to their cabins. But Karen remembers that Carl was never willing to pay for electrical service, probably not only because of the expense, but because the Reichhardt family viewed having no electricity or heat as an adventure; a refreshing change from everyday life. For light they used kerosene lanterns, which Carl placed in every room. He diligently kept the lanterns clean and soot free, and they added to the rustic charm.

When John and Ann Reichhardt and their one-year-old son Aaron moved to Estes Park in 1977 after John graduated from the Palmer College of Chiropractic, they lived at the Wigwam for the summer while they looked for a permanent home and established a Chiropractic practice in Estes Park. The Reichhardts had the practice in Estes Park for 30 years, with Ann as office manager.

A stable and storage shed used to be a fifth building on the Wigwam property. Inside the storage portion of the building were several oversized crates that contained large printed unbound pages of Anna Wolfrom's books. They were unreadable because the sheets of paper had several pages each, completely out of order. In the crawlspace of the Bunkhouse, there were more large crates labeled "Contents: Indian Pottery," showing that they had been used for shipping Anna's purchases for the curio shop. There were crates in the shed too that contained an old Victrola, and clothing and gear from the WWI era that the children tried on and attempted to wear, even though they were much too big.

In the 1980s the stable had deteriorated and some of the weathered siding, which had a nice patina, popular in that era, was stolen. The building had become very unstable, so the Reichhardts tore it down, and preserved the weathered wood siding to be repurposed. John Reichhardt gave this siding,

Exterior view of the Wigwam and driveway from Anna's day.

Same exterior view of the Wigwam and driveway with the Reichhardt's Volvo in front take in the 1980's. In those days, a person could drive a car all the way to the Wigwam. Note the similarities and changes from the earlier photo with the same view, above.

along with the Majestic stove that Anna had used and left at the Wigwam, to Tom Thomas, previous owner of the Notchtop Restaurant in Estes Park, as a trade for a piece of art. The agreement was that he would donate the stove to the Estes Park Museum when he no longer needed it. Anna's Majestic stove sat in the Notchtop for years after that, and they used it as a serving table for coffee and condiments. Thomas eventually sold the Notchtop to Ronn & Michelle Shadows, who upheld the agreement and eventually donated it to the Estes Park Museum, where it resides today. The weathered wood from the stable building is still part of the Notchtop décor, high on the walls in the main dining room.

John & Ann's boys, Aaron and Robin, spent many weekends at the Wigwam with their grand-parents. By that time, the cabin had running water and a bath. The Reichhardts never did have electricity in all the years they lived at the Wigwam. They used a generator sparingly when they wanted to use power tools or had other needs for electricity.

As Carl Reichhardt aged, he wasn't able to maintain the Wigwam as easily, and John and his wife Ann stepped in to help with the ongoing care of the Wigwam buildings. In the last years they owned the property, Carl and Carol only made day trips to the Wigwam.

Eventually it became time for the families to consider what the future of the property should be.

By this time, the older Markus had sold his share of the property to Richard and Bonnie Griebe of Boulder.

There were nine children between Reichhardt and Markus, and although some of those offspring would have undoubtedly liked to keep and use the property, none were able to. It was impractical to split the property in that many directions.

Finally, the families reached the conclusion that the best alternative would be to sell the property for inclusion into Rocky Mountain National Park. The Reichhardt family was happy about this outcome, as they had always advocated for the acquisition and preservation by Rocky Mountain National Park.[69]

Carl Reichhardt and his family created a legacy with their ownership of the Wigwam property. Carl and Carol lovingly restored and maintained the Wigwam cabin, stood firm against selling portions off for development, and instilled a love of the land and a respect for Anna Wolfrom's history in their children. The tradition continued when the younger Reichhardts became adults and treated the Wigwam with the same care and reverence. Even after the family sold the property for inclusion into Rocky Mountain National Park, they continued to care deeply about it, and advocate for it. Because of John Reichhardt's efforts, the Wigwam buildings have not been torn down, and are even being considered for a future adaptive use.

68. Oral Interview with Karen Reichhardt 11/7/17.

69. Oral Interview with John and Ann Reichhardt 10/25/17.

11
CHAPTER

Back to Nature

The Conservation Fund based in Arlington, Virginia, acquired the 160 acres Anna Wolfrom homesteaded for inclusion into Rocky Mountain National Park in 1989. The Fund paid Carl Reichhardt, Henry Markus, and Richard and Bonnie Griebe $290,000 for the acreage. (Markus senior had sold his share to the Griebes by then.) At the same time, the Conservation Fund purchased 309 acres west of Highway 7 adjacent to the Wigwam land called the Baldpate property for $1,550,000. The Wigwam property, also called the Reichhardt property, along with the Baldpate property totaled 469.89 acres.

an island of Park property up until then. The land was officially donated to Rocky Mountain National Park by the Conservation Fund in 1991.

Can you imagine the shores of Lily Lake surrounded by homes? It almost happened.

In 1982, the Larimer County Commissioners reviewed plans for a development across Highway 7 from Lily Lake called Baldpate I, which included 15 lots on 63 acres. The Commissioners denied the proposal on the grounds that it was not consistent with the Larimer County Land Use Plan. But, the developer appealed that decision in Larimer County

Can you imagine the shores of Lily Lake surrounded by homes?
It almost happened.

The Baldpate property is a parcel of land south and west of Lily Mountain on the west side of Highway 7, including Lily Lake. This part of Rocky Mountain National park is about seven miles south of downtown Estes Park on State Highway 7. This acquisition, along with another 59.45 acres on the east side of Highway 7 the Fund acquired in 1992 for $650,000, extended the park's eastern border to connect with the Twin Sisters area, which had been

District Court two years later. The court's decision was that the Larimer County Land Use Plan did not consist of enough incompatibility to deny the project. That sent the project back to the Board of County Commissioners, who then approved it.

The following year, an additional proposal came before Larimer County called Baldpate II, this time for 561 dwelling units, both single and multi-family, on 132 lots. Again, Larimer County Commissioners

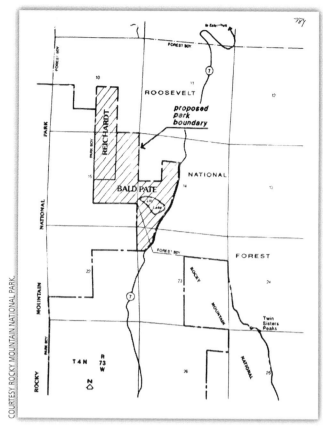

Map of the Baldpate and Reichhardt Acquisition by Rocky Mountain National Park in 1989. Note the rectangle parcel labeled "Reichhardt" is the 160 acres that Anna Wolfrom originally homesteaded.

approved the proposal, subject to several conditions. Of these homes, 161 were to surround Lily Lake.

Rocky Mountain National Park and all the adjacent landowners opposed this development, which thankfully did not happen. The Conservation Fund acted just in time to avoid commercial development.

Not only did this addition to Rocky Mountain National Park preserve pristine and spectacular mountain land, it preserved key habitat areas for the peregrine falcon and a migration route for elk. The building just east of Highway 7 across from Lily Lake, formerly a gift shop operated by the Mace family, then a real estate office, was converted into a Visitor's Center after this acquisition, as a joint effort between the National Park Service and the National Forest Service. Unfortunately this Visitor's Center has since been closed, and the building is now empty.[70]

The Wigwam buildings were slated for demolition by Rocky Mountain National Park in 1993.[71] There were many years when it was common practice for any buildings acquired by Rocky Mountain National Park to be torn down. It takes money and resources to maintain buildings, and the thinking of park officials for years was that the land should be brought back to its natural state. Besides that, access to the Wigwam was and still is difficult, with no road available for public use.

The same year the buildings were to be demolished, John Reichhardt contacted the Colorado Historical Society, asking if they could be re-evaluated for inclusion into the National Historic Register. Prior to Reichhardt's request, the Wigwam buildings had been determined in 1991 by the Colorado Historical Society to be *not* eligible for inclusion into the National Register.

Letters from 1993 illustrate John's attempts to have it included on the National Historic Register and the reluctance of park officials to do so. Despite documentation provided by Reichhardt and others explaining the significance of Anna Wolfrom's accomplishments as the first independent woman homesteader in the Estes Valley and her success as a businesswoman both at the Wigwam and in Estes Park, the Park Historian argued against Anna's significance as a historical figure. Homer Rouse, the Superintendent at the time, was also reluctant to cooperate in recognizing the Wigwam buildings as historically significant.[72]

Nevertheless, the Colorado Historical Society investigated the matter again in 1993 and declared that the Wigwam buildings *were* eligible for inclusion into the National Historic Register, the same year the park had scheduled the demolition of the buildings. Because of the efforts of John Reichhardt, the buildings were saved, but this was not the last time they would be threatened.

According to a historian at the Colorado State Historical Office, the buildings are still eligible today and could be brought forward for formal inclusion into the National Register. This would,

Vandalism to the Wigwam in May of 1996.

however, take the cooperation and support of Rocky Mountain National Park.

⟨◦⟩

Despite being a new acquisition for Rocky Mountain National Park in 1989, officials virtually ignored the Wigwam buildings for 10 years before any repairs or maintenance were done. During those years, vandals took their toll. College kids came there to party, and left beer cans and other debris. The dilapidated cabins surrounded by trash were encountered by others who assumed correctly that the cabins were uncared for, and figured they were deteriorating shacks that needed tearing down.

In May of 1996, one incident of vandalism topped all the rest. These vandals broke into all four buildings, took a pick axe and methodically went through, destroying everything they could. They broke out windows, and chopped through doors and roofs, and shattered the toilet and sink into jagged pieces. They shot holes in the siding, and ripped out anything of value. Soon afterward, a hiker saw the damage and notified the Reichhardts. Even though the property was no longer theirs, the family was devastated at the damage. Who would want to destroy the Wigwam?

The buildings were vandalized so extensively that the National Park would have torn them down as a matter of course if it weren't for the involvement of the Colorado Historical Society and John Reichhardt. It took a long time before the damage was repaired. The buildings were left open for rodents who invaded and added to the destruction. Over time, all of the buildings deteriorated from a combination of neglect, rodent infestations, leaking roofs, and vandals. [73]

For many years, John Reichhardt was the sole researcher and advocate for preserving the history of Anna Wolfrom Dove and the Wigwam Tea

The Wigwam interior after being stabilized in 2005 & 2006. This project was made possible by the Rocky Mountain Nature Association under the direction of Curt Buchholtz.

some newspaper articles about her. Redman was kind enough to donate the diary to the Estes Park Museum, to the delight of Lynn Swain, then curator of the museum. Reichhardt then did some research and put together a timeline of the most significant events in Anna Wolfrom's life from Estes Park newspapers and public records. [74]

In a lucky twist of fate, an unidentified man found a few photo albums in a dumpster in Denver.

In a lucky twist of fate, an unidentified man found a few photo albums in a dumpster in Denver. These albums contained historic photos of Estes Park, one of which contained pictures of Anna Wolfrom and the Wigwam.

Room. Reichhardt's first source of information was John Redman, whose father Thomas Redman had been one of the partners who purchased the Wigwam property from Anna in 1948. Thomas Redman visited the Wigwam during the year that Karen Reichhardt lived there. He and Karen talked about Anna during that visit, and Redman told her he had some information about Anna.

Fourteen years later, John Reichhardt contacted Redman at his New York office, who confirmed he had Anna's diary in his possession and copies of

These albums contained historic photos of Estes Park, one of which contained pictures of Anna Wolfrom and the Wigwam. This person had the foresight to donate the albums to the Estes Park Museum, and museum staff then alerted John Reichhardt.

After obtaining these old photographs of the Wigwam, Reichhardt put together a slide show and lecture on Anna Wolfrom that he presented locally in Estes Park several times. He also compiled a brief written history of Anna's life, and donated it to the

Estes Park Museum. Had it not been for his efforts, most of the history about Anna Wolfrom Dove and the Wigwam Tea Room would have been lost.

Curt Buchholtz, former executive director of the Rocky Mountain Nature Association, also advocated for the Wigwam. In 2005, the Rocky Mountain Nature Association, under the direction of Buchholtz, raised the money that it took to finally repair and stabilize the buildings. It took $107,819 of donor money to stabilize and repair the Wigwam buildings. In the fall of 2005 and spring of 2006, crews spent several weeks cleaning and stabilizing the interior of the Wigwam, sealing it up to prevent rodents, and repairing the roof. Stabilizing the building involved installing an extensive roof bracing system of 2 × 4's inside the building to prevent collapse. Then, during the summer of 2007, the three remaining buildings were stabilized and mothballed. [75]

The same historian who confirmed the Wigwam's eligibility for the National Historic Register also said that, as federally owned property, Rocky Mountain National Park must consult with the Colorado Historical Society as required by Section 106 of the National Historic Preservation Act before any alterations can be made to the buildings, i.e. a new roof, etc. The Park Service could decide to tear the buildings down, but it would involve many layers of approval and would be an involved process. This is why the buildings are still standing today.

From the time Anna Wolfrom built the road to the Wigwam around 1914 until after Rocky Mountain National Park acquired it, the public could access the Wigwam and beyond from Aspen Brook Road, also known as the Wind River Trail, which met Highway 66 just south of the entrance to Windcliff. That road still exists, but is gated and posted with No Trespassing signs. (Note: there is another newer road called Aspen Brook Road off Highway 66, near the Dunraven Restaurant, different from the original Aspen Brook Road.) The original Aspen Brook Road was historically a trail and

The gate on Aspen Brook Road that property owners put up to stop public access.

road called the Wind River Trail that has existed since the early 1900s, providing public access to the Wind River Valley, Lily Lake, and beyond. Adding to the confusion, there is another nearby trail called the Wind River Trail that originates next to the mouth of the Alva B. Adams Tunnel, just across Highway 66, and goes south from there.

Many years ago, Don and Wylene Buser, the Windcliff developers, and the families who owned properties on Aspen Brook Road battled in court over access. The Busers wanted to use Aspen Brook Road for access to their development. The court ruled in favor of the landowners, who were allowed to continue prohibiting public access via Aspen Brook Road to Windcliff residents. As a result, the Windcliff developers built a second road, just north of Aspen Brook Road, for access to their development.

After many incidents of vandalism, break-ins, trespassing and illegal camping, the landowners along Aspen Brook Road put up a gate and began actively prohibiting public thoroughfare. Property owners were able to pass through to access their properties, but they denied access to anyone else. Some of the property owners were diligent about shooing people away who attempted to pass through, and gradually over time the use of that access road became less and less.

Today, Aspen Brook Road/Wind River Trail closest to the Wigwam is nearly grown over because it has been rarely used for many years. Some people believe that since Rocky Mountain National Park is a federal agency, owned by the public, that this could be interpreted that we are all landowners in that area and should have access to the Wigwam via this route. Rocky Mountain National Park could have taken this matter to court to try to preserve public access via Aspen Brook Road, but officials have never pursued it. Fortunately, there is public access from Lily Lake to the Wigwam, but it is more than twice the distance than via Highway 66.

⊰••⊱

It's been many years since the Park stabilized and mothballed the Wigwam buildings, and there are no future plans for restoration. According to Vaughn Baker, Superintendent of Rocky Mountain National Park from 2002-2015, the reason why the Wigwam buildings have never been restored is because of the lack of access. Since there is no longer any way for the public to drive all the way there, he says it is difficult to find a new use for the buildings. Finding a use is key to finding funds for restoration.

An example of this are the buildings at the McGraw Ranch, just north of Estes Park off of Devil's Gulch Road. After acquisition of the ranch in the early 1990s by Rocky Mountain National Park, the ranch buildings were slated to be torn down. But the National Trust for Historic Preservation raised money to restore the McGraw Ranch buildings, to the tune of several million dollars. The driving force behind this was a planned use for these buildings. After a thorough renovation, they are now used as a scientific research facility by the national park.

It's been proven that the Wigwam buildings are historically significant, so the Park continues to maintain them. Workers installed a new asphalt shingle roof on the Wigwam during the summer of 2014. But for the most part, the buildings are ignored, and most of the general public who visit Rocky Mountain National Park never learn about the Wigwam. At the very least, a plaque or commemorative sign could be installed at the Wigwam explaining the history of Anna Wolfrom Dove and the Wigwam Tea Room, and Anna's many contributions to the Estes Park area.

If funds could be allocated for refurbishing, the Wigwam buildings could be used to re-enact history, like is done at the Holzwarth Historic Homestead on the west side of Rocky Mountain National Park. There, park employees dress up in traditional period costumes and greet visitors, showing the public what homesteading life was like in that day and age. Accessing the Holzwarth Historic Homestead requires a hike across a meadow of about ¼ mile. Why not offer a lengthier hike to the Wigwam for interested park visitors? There are undoubtedly plenty who would make the trek. Rocky Mountain National Park recently announced plans to build a new trail connecting the Wigwam to Highway 66, making this entirely possible with a new shorter route. What a novelty it would be if people could visit the Wigwam and find park volunteers reenacting the tea room operation at the Wigwam, even allowing visitors to purchase refreshments and enjoy the setting, the same as they were able to 100 years ago.

The American cultural atmosphere today, more than ever, is increasingly open to recognizing women and their contributions. The timing may be just right for more public knowledge and recognition of Anna Wolfrom Dove and her unique contributions to early Estes Valley life. Anna's memory and the Wigwam buildings deserve to receive greater attention. But currently, most visitors never learn about the Wigwam, unless they are educated about Anna and her tea room from a well-informed local resident. Members of the public should have the chance to learn about Anna and the Wigwam Tea Room when they visit Rocky Mountain National Park.

70. Rocky Mountain National Park Archives, Tract Records, File Unit #190, Tract #07-143.

71. Letter from Patricia K. Childs to Mr. Lane Ittelson, Colorado Historical Society, January 28, 1993.

72. Correspondence between RMNP Officials and the Colorado State Historical Society, March 23, 1993, April 19, 1993, February 1, 1994.

73. Oral interview with Curt Buchholtz 7/11/17.

74. Correspondence between John Redman and John Reichhardt, November 20, 1989, April 20, 1990, Undated, and January 9, 1991.

75. Rocky Mountain Nature Association Quarterly, March 2006.

12
CHAPTER

The Wigwam Today

The Wigwam cabin, the original Homestead Cabin, Anna's residence cabin, and the bunkhouse are all still standing along Aspen Brook in Rocky Mountain National Park. It always was an out-of-the-way location, and it still is, even more so.

The only public access to the Wigwam is from Lily Lake, but the trail is not marked. To get there, park at Lily Lake or the lot across State Hwy 7 from Lily Lake. Walk south from Lily Lake on the trail next to (west of) Highway 7 to a clearing in the trees, and turn west, following the Storm Pass trail downhill in a southwest direction. After following the trail downhill about ½ mile through a thick forest, you will come to a bridge where the trail crosses Aspen Brook. Just before the bridge, take a sharp

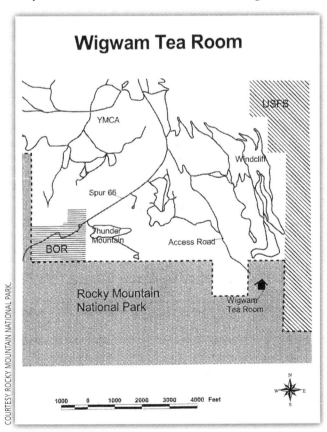

Map of the area surrounding the Wigwam property, now part of Rocky Mountain National Park.

The trail from Lily Lake to the Wigwam is not marked. You will see this sign after you turn north, leaving the Storm Pass trail.

119

The new trail to the Wigwam that was constructed after the flood of 2013 washed out much of the old trail. The new trail is higher up on the side of the hill.

right (leaving the Storm Pass Trail) and head north. The sign there indicates that the trail does not continue, and there is no public access in 1.7 miles, but there is no sign directing you to the Wigwam.

Continue north on this trail past the sign. The flood of 2013 washed out Aspen Brook Road, and damaged much of the trail leading to the Wigwam from Lily Lake. In 2017 and 2018, crews repaired and moved a portion of the washed out trail which used to follow Aspen Brook more closely. The new trail is further uphill, east of Aspen Brook, and there are now a handful of switchbacks. When you get close to the Wigwam, you can see the old logging road down below, before the switchbacks bring you down to meet it. Continue for a short distance on the flat two-track road, and soon you'll be at the Wigwam. The Wigwam site is about two miles from Lily Lake.

The remains of Jimmy Fields' cabin are near the meadow on the way to the Wigwam. Look for the hitch rack on the southwest corner of this meadow, and the remains are just above it, to the west at the edge of the trees. Since the flood of 2013, the trail no longer goes through the meadow, but what's left of his cabin is clearly visible at the edge of the meadow from the new trail.

For Windcliff homeowners and those who have permission for access from Windcliff, the Wigwam is only about ¼ mile from the southernmost point of Eaglecliff Circle Drive, and is shown on the Windcliff neighborhood map. There is a pullout with room for one or two cars to park on the roadside where the trail begins.

Some hikers still access the Wigwam via Aspen Brook Road/Wind River Trail off Highway 66. However, this route now crosses private property and you will be trespassing if you use this route without permission.

While most people who visit the Estes Park area don't know about the Wigwam, there are many locals who do, and many who feel Anna Wolfrom Dove's history is important and worth preserving.

Pamalah Tipps, a resident of neighboring Windcliff Estates, organized a group of Windcliff residents to celebrate the 100th Anniversary of the

A group from Windcliff who commemorated the 100 year anniversary of the opening of the Wigwam Tea Room in 2014, with a specially packaged picnic lunch and a formal presentation about Anna's life.

opening of Anna Wolfrom's Wigwam Tea Room in July of 2014. Carrying boxed picnic lunches prepared and labeled especially for the occasion, the group hiked to the Wigwam, where a brief history of Anna's life was read aloud by Stephen Tipps, and several others read quotes by Anna Wolfrom, pertaining to her experience at the Wigwam. Pamalah Tipps explains that "Everyone knew of Anna, but perhaps not in such detail before the picnic. All are gratified that the Park Service has kept the buildings from falling down in ruins."

Outside the gatehouse at the entrance to Windcliff Estates, there are signs describing Anna Wolfrom, Frank Webster, and Don and Wylene Buser and the significant impact they all had on the area. The folks at the Windcliff office are Anna Wolfrom fans, and many Windcliff residents regularly hike to the Wigwam and beyond. A popular hike among Windcliff residents and visitors is past the Wigwam, up to Lily Lake, and finally to the Baldpate Inn for lunch.

Sarah Donohoe, Hikemaster at the YMCA of the Rockies for most years between 2004 and 2018, has regularly led hiking groups to the Wigwam each summer. She described Anna's original claim cabin as being "only a pile of lumber" when she first started leading hikes in 2004. During their visits, Sarah and her hiking group would investigate the cabin remains and the other three buildings while discussing Anna's "adventurous and fearless spirit, her strength as a single woman living alone in the wilderness . . . the hospitality she extended . . . and her entrepreneurial nature."

One particular hike in 2014, both Sarah and Keith Pritchard, a volunteer YMCA Hikemaster, remember as being particularly memorable. A group of about ten hikers were sitting on the hillside eating their lunch above the Wigwam when someone noticed movement in the tall grass below the road. It turned out to be a very large shaggy cinnamon bear, who ambled around within the group's sight for about half an hour before disappearing. This led Sarah to reflect on what it was like for Anna Wolfrom when she was alone at the Wigwam and likely encountered bears, coyotes, mountain goats, and elk.

To honor Anna's memory and celebrate the tea room history, Sarah occasionally surprised hikers

Cinnamon bear that was captured with a telephoto lens on one of many hikes to the Wigwam led by hike masters from the YMCA of the Rockies.

by serving them hot tea and cookies when they stopped for a break at the Wigwam. On one occasion, Sarah remembers that she "snuck away from the group as they scattered to explore the historic structures, and when I reappeared, I wore a long skirt and carried a carafe of hot tea. I spread out two picnic blankets next to the tea room, poured tea, and served lemon cookies and Oreos. (The Oreo cookie was first produced in 1912). The hikers were surprised and delighted with our impromptu tea. We made sure to extend our pinky fingers as we sipped our tea and we politely nibbled on our 'biscuits' as we talked of life during the days of the Wigwam Tea Room."

⥱⬥⥱

I wish I'd been able to relax on the Wigwam porch enjoying some tea and scrumptious cakes, and visit with Anna Wolfrom. I can imagine her smile as she pours steaming hot water into a china teacup, and her purposeful stride as she moves around the Wigwam, checking to make sure all the candies and cakes are lined up in perfect order on their tiered trays.

Anna's tenacity, intelligence, loyalty and work ethic were remarkable. She was a devoted daughter, sister, aunt and wife who enriched her family's lives. Anna displayed exceptional courage to undertake the filing of a homestead claim in the rugged wilderness, and beyond that, to operate all of her businesses with a profit and a smile.

813R00068

Made in the USA
Lexington, KY
02 July 2019